Gareth Heaton

# Do Maintain

How to sharpen knives,
scissors and garden tools.

Do Book Co

For Dad

Published by
The Do Book Company 2025
Works in Progress Publishing Ltd
**thedobook.co**



5 per cent of our proceeds from the sale of this book is given to The DO Lectures to help it achieve its aim of making positive change: thedolectures.com

A CIP catalogue record for this book is available from the British Library

ISBN 978-1-914168-64-2

10 9 8 7 6 5 4 3 2

To find out more about our company, books and authors, please visit **thedobook.co** or follow us **@dobookco**

Cover designed by James Victore
Book designed and set by Ratiotype
Printed and bound in the EU by OZGraf on Munken, an FSC® certified paper
GPSR: productsafety@thedobook.co

MIX
Paper | Supporting responsible forestry
FSC® C163799

Disclaimer: The information in this book has been compiled by way of general guidance in relation to the specific subject addressed, but is not a substitute and not to be relied on for medical, healthcare or other professional advice on specific circumstances and in specific locations. Every precaution must be taken when using, working with and maintaining sharp objects, including but not limited to kitchen knives. When sharpening always have a first-aid kit close to hand and seek medical help if needed. The author and publishers disclaim, as far as the laws allow, any liability arising directly or indirectly from the use, or misuse, of the information contained in this book.

# Contents

# Foreword



**'It takes time, you just have to stay with it', he said, this bright-eyed, bushy-bearded man called Gareth (Gaz) Heaton in his warmly lit shop on a cold day in Yorkshire. I was learning how to sharpen my knives alongside a group of men I'd never met before.**

Sharpening a knife and tending to your mental health have more in common than you might think. Both demand presence and a certain kind of tenderness. Consistency, care and attention. At first, yeah, it's clunky. You're following steps, hoping you're doing it right. But slowly, the process starts to work on you as much as you're working on it. It becomes a kind of ritual.

In a culture that prioritises quick fixes, there is a tendency to dispose of, instead of maintain. But there's something quietly rebellious about maintaining something. Sharpening. Caring. *Staying with it.* In a world that's obsessed with getting more, being faster, starting fresh—maintenance is the quieter, wiser, older sibling. It's the part of us that says, 'actually, this thing is still good. It just needs a bit of attention.'

There could be a whole book written on bilateral stimulation and knife sharpening: the gentle to-and-fro that can help calm the nervous system, quiet the mind, and bring us back into our body. But really, in simple terms, it's about *doing* something small that points to something big.

Perhaps that's why Admiral William McRaven's commencement speech resonated with millions, and his quote: 'If you want to change the world, start off by making your bed'. In this context, I'd say: if you want to change and maintain your life, start by sharpening your knife.

As a therapist, I talk about mental maintenance a lot. It's not about fixing yourself; you're not broken. But about approaching life with intentionality. That's the gift of maintenance. It's not just the result: the sharp knife, the calmer mind, the better day — it's the practice. The doing. The moment you choose to tend to something instead of replacing it. When you stop rushing and start paying attention. That's where the good shit lives.

We see it in the therapy room all the time. The people who lean into regular maintenance (rather than waiting for a crisis) tend to live with more steadiness. More self-awareness. More room for joy. They know that care isn't a one-time thing; it's something you build, slowly, over time.

So, take this as a little invitation. As you sharpen your tools, consider what else in your life might benefit from the same gentle rhythm. A friendship. A feeling. Your nervous system. What if you didn't wait until it broke? What if the act of maintenance *is* the point?

You don't have to overhaul everything. You just have to begin. Find poetry in the ordinary. Move slowly. Do it with care. And trust that over time, you'll feel more like yourself again, not because something was wrong, but because you finally gave it your attention.

**Chance Marshall**, co-founder of Self Space

WE SHARPEN KNIVES
CUTLERY
OPEN
10-5
TUES-SAT
WE SHARPEN KNIVES
31

# Introduction

**People I meet often assume I must be an obsessive, lifelong knife sharpener who's been honing his craft since he was a young lad. The truth is that up until my late thirties, I was very much like the majority of the people who attend the sharpening classes I now teach — probably like you are too. I was keen, had some basic equipment, but lacked the knowledge and direction needed to do a good job.**

I always saw the benefit of having sharp knives and tools, I even made the occasional effort to keep them sharp. But I didn't really know how to do it properly, nor did I fully appreciate the benefits, until about six years ago.

Up until that point I had done a surprising amount of different jobs — and lasted about three years in each. I never felt like I was searching for something magical. I always enjoyed the work I did, I just moved on when it felt like the right time.

Then, in one big cliché, it all changed in an instant. This was back in 2019 and at the time I was working as a self-employed gardener, the thing I had studied and done on and off over the years. On this particular day, I was mowing a lawn and listening to a podcast called *The Side Hustle Project*. The guest was a bloke from the US called

Matt who had just left the military and started a knife-sharpening business. I listened with great interest as Matt talked about how he'd learned to sharpen knives properly, had sharpened for free to practise and build a reputation, and how he had managed to turn this into a business.

Straight away I thought to myself, 'I'm having a bit of this'—albeit as a new side project. I gave some thought to whether I could make it work financially, and how to prevent it from going the same way as all my previous 'projects'. Maybe I was getting ahead of myself but, like I say, it struck a chord.

There are almost 30 million households in the UK, as well as cafés, bars, restaurants and hotels, all with at least one single kitchen knife to work with—most with many more. So, I thought to myself, *surely* there must be demand for someone to sharpen them for local homes and businesses? I certainly hadn't seen anyone else doing it. I couldn't help thinking that if you add scissors and tools to the mix, there must be loads of work out there.

Well, I can confirm that there *is* a load of sharpening to do out there, but I don't need to tell you that. You've probably got a pile of stuff that needs sharpening, which presumably is why you're reading this book.

---

In the early stages of my sharpening journey, I sharpened as many knives for free as I could get my hands on. I obsessively watched YouTube videos to try and understand the nuances of sharpening, decipher what it was I was being told, and try to separate the good advice from the bad. Within a few months, I'd had a batch of flyers printed and posted them around the local area, advertising to all that 'Grinderman Sharpening Services' was in operation.

When someone got in touch to express an interest in using the sharpening service, they were sent a message containing the combination code for the padlock on our out-house and instructions on how to carry out a drop-off. They could turn up at their convenience, place their labelled items in one of a stack of boxes on the left, and inform me they'd been. I'd then sharpen their knife at home before placing it back in a box on the right for collection. It worked perfectly, and I gradually began to build up my customer base.

Over the next few months, I dropped a day a week of gardening to keep up with the demand from new customers. I flitted from sharpening in the back yard to sharpening in the kitchen when the weather got too bad.

Fast-forward five years, and the sharpening business is no longer the embryonic idea it was as I mowed the lawn, listening to a podcast. With my partner Georgina, we leased a shop and opened 'Community Cutlery' (it was George who convinced me to change the name from Grinderman Sharpening Services and I'm forever grateful that she did!).

I'm pleased to say that at the time of writing we're a thriving small business. Shortly after opening we began working with a handful of knife and kitchenware suppliers from the UK, Spain, Germany, France and Japan. And we sharpen thousands of items a year: for the local community, for cooks and chefs in their places of work, and for anyone else who fancies using our 'Sharpening via post' service.

So, at the risk of losing all the customers I've built up over the last few years, I'm going to share everything I know about knife sharpening and proper maintenance. I believe it's something we should all learn to do and am passionate about getting as many people as possible sharpening and properly looking after their tools and utensils.

CHAPTER ONE

# Why we need to sharpen

**When you sharpen for a living, you have a lot of time to think, and those thoughts often end up being about sharpening and why it's a good idea to keep your tools sharp.**

Let's start with knives. Kitchen knives especially are the one thing that causes the most frustration to users when they're dull or blunt. The experience of reaching for a knife to prepare your veg and the edge being so dull that it doesn't even slice the flesh is ubiquitous. You're in the kitchen, just about to get the dinner on, you reach for the knife and it doesn't even cut the skin of your tomato. You start to feel the stress level rising: 'Man, this knife is driving me mad.'

You take the tip of the knife and jab it in to get your cut started, you then place the cutting edge of the knife onto the pierced hole and force it through the vegetable. As you repeat this, the knife slips.

'THIS ******* KNIFE!'

From the next room: 'What?'

'Oh, nothing, I was just saying, this knife, it's terrible.'

'Oh yeah, it's bad, isn't it?'

'We need to get it sharpened.'

You carry on, hacking your way through whatever ingredients

you're preparing until the meal is ready, at which point you immediately forget about the knife. Sharpening it never re-enters your head until the next time it's called into action, at which point the story repeats itself. Day in, day out, until eventually the knife goes in the bin.

'Right, that's it, we're getting a new knife.'

---

Great, lovely. Taking a new knife out of the box is a dream, *for now*! Because, guess what, this knife is only going to end up in the same state as the last one if it isn't maintained. Any knife, no matter how expensive it is, is going to need maintaining. It's something that can't be avoided.

You can make a blunt knife work but when it's sharp it's going to do the job you ask of it so much better. When someone who's been using a dull knife for years tries a newly sharpened blade it almost makes them giddy! We see it in the shop every day. The knife glides through a carrot with so little resistance that their mouth falls open wide enough to pop in a whole Spanish onion. There's an intake of breath, a smile, a look to their partner: 'Oh wow, John, you've got to try this!'

Using a kitchen knife that is sharp is a truly joyful experience, especially if you've laboured on with something blunt for so long. But banishing frustrations and making your experience more joyful isn't the only benefit of using a sharp knife. It's also going to:

— Make cooking and preparing food quicker and safer
— Save you money on replacement knives
— Improve the quality of your chopped ingredients

This last point I find particularly impressive. If you use a sharp knife, you're doing less cellular damage to the food you're cutting. So rather than mashing and crushing your way through the item, your sharp knife with its thin, consistent edge disturbs far fewer cells, helping to maintain flavour and slow the rate of oxidation.

The same goes for any tool with an edge. If its sharpness is its function, then it needs to be maintained. Dull scissors will crease paper or snag material. Blunt secateurs will require an excessive amount of force to use. A neglected axe is going to slip or bounce and risk causing serious injury.

While the benefits might not be completely obvious to everyone, the pitfalls of using blunt tools must be. The excessive effort, frustrations and unsatisfactory results are undeniable. So why is it that more of us don't address the issue? Why does such a large percentage of the population labour on in this way?

I've given this a lot of thought and here's what I've come up with. We can break these people down into several groups:

— **Group 1:** The people who simply don't know about sharpening. It's never crossed their mind that knives can be maintained, nobody has mentioned it to them, and they've never seen a sharpening service when they're out and about.

— **Group 2:** They are aware of sharpening but financially it just isn't a priority.

— **Group 3:** They are aware of sharpening, they can afford it, but they never remember to arrange to get it done, or else they do remember but just can't be bothered.

Personally, I think the third group is the biggest. On a daily basis, George and I speak to customers who confess that they've been thinking about bringing their knives in for a sharpen but never get around to it. So why is it so hard to remember to do this? Or why don't some people even know that things can be sharpened? Surely the daily use of a blunt knife must be indication enough that something isn't right?

I've not got a convincing answer to these questions but what I do know for sure is that this hasn't always been the case. In days gone by, there was a far stronger culture of looking after one's possessions; people couldn't afford to keep replacing their tools — so they looked after them. They were maintained and sharpened as a matter of course.

Often this would be done by one of the many itinerant sharpeners plying their trade up and down streets across the UK. Calling out, 'Knives to grind!' to attract the attention of local residents. The sharpeners would be inundated with kitchen knives and scissors, which they'd sharpen right there on the street with the use of their pedal-powered grinding wheels (and it seems this exact service is still in operation in many parts of the world today).

So, what happened between then and now to foster such a negative attitude shift? Why has this approach fallen from favour?

For starters, I know that a market flooded with mass-produced, cheap knives and tools doesn't help. A quick online search shows I can buy a 'high-end' chef's knife for £2.44 ($3.17) including international shipping. *Including international shipping!* That's about the same price as sending a letter within the UK, and almost exactly the same price we charge to sharpen two inches of a knife.

With these prices, it's little wonder that the average knife user doesn't feel encouraged to spend money or time sharpening their own. And at this price it matters little that the quality is poor — they can just be used then replaced. But what of the environmental cost? Hundreds of thousands, if not millions, of plastic-handled, short life-expectancy knives being disposed of can't be a good thing for anyone — except the companies making them.

So is it too late to change this attitude? Not for you! Let's face it, unless you were handed this book by your friends at an intervention staged because of your excessive purchasing of cheap kitchen knives, it's highly likely that you're already motivated to learn how to sharpen (or improve what you already know), so you aren't part of the problem. As for the whole broken system, I really don't know what the solution is there; I'm just a knife sharpener with too much thinking time...

But what I do know is that visibility helps. When we set up Community Cutlery, we knew that if we wanted the sharpening service to take off it needed a public face. People needed to walk or drive past it every day until they were finally compelled to bring their knives in! And we knew that after doing it once, the benefits would speak for themselves.

As a home sharpener looking after your own knives, you'll be removing those blunt knife frustrations and making your life easier. You'll be learning a new skill and reducing the amount of cheap knives going into landfill. If you want to do a bit extra, extol the virtues of sharpening and using a sharp knife to your friends. Let them try yours when they're round at your house, slag theirs off when you're round at theirs. And hey, just a thought here, but why not buy them this book!

Gaz and George in the shop

CHAPTER TWO

# What's a whetstone? And other FAQs

**Over the years I've had the pleasure of teaching hundreds of people how to sharpen their tools. More often than not they've had a crack at it before—they've got the equipment and the desire, but for some reason it didn't take.**

There are the obvious technical issues and fears people have, which we'll address in Chapter 4, but for now we'll have a look at other barriers to you becoming a long-term sharpener. So here's a few frequently asked questions.

1.

## How much experience do I need to learn how to sharpen?

None! If you're coming to this without the first clue of how to sharpen then that's absolutely fine. The instructions in the book are designed with a complete beginner in mind.

In the early days, although I 'knew' how to sharpen I wasn't convinced I *really* knew how to sharpen. So I set about—along with the help of YouTube—teaching myself how to do it properly. And you know what? It was a pain.

I found so much conflicting information, so many videos used words that assumed prior knowledge, meaning I had to piece together what I learned from countless videos just to get a handle on what I was meant to be doing.

What I'm getting at here is that I know what it's like to be a beginner, to be unsure about 'bevels' and 'angles' and to wish all the information was in one place. It's what led me to start running workshops. And that's what this book is all about. By the end, you should have a very clear idea of what's involved and how to do it.

## 2.

## How physically demanding is it?

Sharpening isn't hugely physical but it does require effort. You probably won't get out of breath but it is likely to make your arms ache a bit at the beginning. As with any new activity, you'll probably be calling on muscles to work in a slightly different way than they do usually, so expect a little fatigue in the hands, arms and shoulders but not much else. And obviously, the bigger the tool you're sharpening (we get into garden spades in Chapter 6!), the more physical it will be.

I do recommend that you sharpen standing up, particularly when working on knives, as it helps to have your weight over the work area, but it's not essential. So if for whatever reason you're unable to stand for an extended period, feel free to sit, but try and get as high as you can next to the surface you're working on.

Over the years, we've had several students attend workshops with physical impairments and it has never meant that they were unable to participate and get the results they'd hoped for. If, while reading the sharpening directions in the book, you see something that you feel you'll be unable to carry out, then please do modify the technique as needed. As long as you achieve the steps that have been laid out there are no rules about how you get there; I'm just relaying the way I think will be easiest.

One thing you're going to need is a little coordination—this one can't be avoided! So, if you feel that coordination is something you might struggle with, then my advice is to take your time (there are no prizes for sharpening a knife in under five minutes), enjoy the process and allow yourself to become comfortable with the techniques involved. As muscle memory builds, so too will your confidence and speed.



3.

## How much time am I going to need to dedicate to this?

Like any new activity, you'll get better with practice, so a certain investment of time will be required. That said, you aren't going to need to quit your job (although I did!).

It's impossible to say exactly how long it's going to take for you to feel comfortable sharpening. Certainly there will be some effort to learn, but almost all students go away feeling confident to sharpen under their own steam after a two-hour lesson. It might take a bit longer for you, as a classroom environment is more intensive, but not much. For the first year or so of my sharpening life I used to allow around 15 minutes a knife, now I'd expect to sharpen an 8-inch chef knife by hand in around five minutes.

The initial period of learning aside, once you've got

your knives back to a good state of repair and have a system of maintenance in place, you'll probably be looking at sharpening them around three times a year, so it won't be a huge demand on your time. Tools, scissors and bread knives will most likely be on a less frequent schedule.

4.

## What equipment will I need and how much is it going to cost?

As affordability is relative, it's difficult to say what you might find an acceptable financial cost for tackling your sharpening jobs at home. But I'll break down some rough costs and you can decide for yourself.

At this stage it's worth mentioning that what you *need* for sharpening and what extras you could buy for sharpening are two different things. So here we're only going to look at the essentials. If further down the line you become obsessed with sharpening and want to furnish yourself with a dozen whetstones, a plethora of honing compounds and a top-of-the-range lapping plate, then go for it. But be assured, as a home sharpener, looking to maintain your own knives and tools at home, you don't need much equipment at all. Here's what you will need, and if you don't know what half these things are, don't worry, we're about to get into all that!

## For knives

- **Combination whetstone:** £40–60 ($50–80). Cheaper options are available but to be avoided.
- **Strop:** £10–30 ($15–40)
- **Lapping stone:** £10–20 ($15–30). Used to keep your whetstones flat.

That's it! There are a couple more things you need that we'll cover later, but you'll almost certainly have them at home already.

## Extras you'll need for scissors, tools and bread knives

- **Marker pen:** £1 ($1.30)
- **Vice:** £20–30 ($25–40). I prefer the smaller articulating kind, but you could definitely manage with a table vice if you already have one.
- **Retractable diamond pen file:** £4–8 for two ($5–10)
- **Tapered 6-inch diamond file:** £8–16 ($10–20)
- **Round or half-round file:** £8–15 ($10–20)

As you can see, there are definitely some costs involved but it shouldn't be an inordinate amount. And remember, we're saving money by doing it ourselves and not buying new knives!

For example, if we compare the cost of the knife-sharpening equipment to the cost of getting them sharpened by a professional sharpening service, £60–110 ($80–140), it's going to get you around ten to twenty knives sharpened.

If you have five knives, that's only between two and four sharpens of each one. You're quids in here!

If, on the other hand, you compare it to the cost of an at-home sharpening device, the most popular 'rolling-type' sharpener on the market is currently retailing at around £160 ($208) and is neither as versatile, nor as effective, as sharpening on a whetstone.

5.

## What is a whetstone and why are we using this method?

Now, in case you're unfamiliar with what a whetstone is (trust me, you'll be well acquainted soon enough!) it's an abrasive block used for the purpose of sharpening knives and tools. We'll go into much more detail in the next chapter. But for now, why aren't we going to be using a less fussy method to sharpen our knives? There are loads of options out there — is there actually anything wrong with them? Is this just whetstone snobbery?

To put it simply, all methods of sharpening were not created equal. In fact, the cynic inside me might even say that some methods of sharpening were created so unequally that they could be considered a 'cash grab' by the companies selling them, rather than an efficient way to sharpen your knives.

If you've ever bought a set of knives which includes any type of sharpening device, it's almost certainly designed to add perceived value and encourage you to make the purchase, rather than to help you maintain the knives going forward. Let's have a quick look at the sharpening options out there and I'll give you my thoughts.

## Steels

This is your absolute classic, an abrasive metal rod on a handle. The thing you think of when you imagine a butcher sharpening up their knife before getting to work.

Steels have been around for so long because they work, to some extent. In the right hands, a good-quality steel has the ability to remove material from a knife's bevel (and yes, you'll soon know what a 'bevel' is) and help to maintain its edge, *but* they are not a good option for sharpening. Most steels sold today, particularly the ones that come with a set of knives, are absolutely useless. They really are just another handle sticking out of the knife block to encourage you to part with your money.

Cheap steels like these are usually very coarse, can leave a poor edge and, if used with too much vigour, can easily leave a knife in a worse state than it was before. The user has far less control over the sharpening angle than when using a whetstone. And it's unlikely to remove material from the entire edge of the knife at the same rate —which is what we'll be doing.

## Pull-through sharpening devices

These come in all shapes and sizes—some have ceramic sharpening wheels, some have tungsten carbide prongs, and some are electric. Either way, they all involve pulling your knife through a slot while the device is braced to the work surface. Some are better than others, but none are very good. Why? Because they remove too much material from your knife, which can drastically shorten its life span. Prolonged use will almost certainly result in an uneven and often chipped and damaged bevel. Repairing knives that have been damaged by this type of sharpener is something we do daily in our workshop. And they only sharpen at one or two pre-set angles, depriving you of the freedom to sharpen a range of knives with differing angles or change the angle if needed.

The worst of the pull-through offenders are the small round ones that usually attach to your work surface with suction cups. If you've got one of these, I urge you to part with it now, as these are truly awful. The tungsten carbide prongs that are responsible for 'sharpening' will literally scrape material from the bevel, leaving a rough, often grooved finish, which is terrible to use.

## Rolling sharpeners

The new kids on the block, and in my opinion the best of the options I've covered so far, but also — you guessed it — not recommended by me. To highlight why, here's a brief anecdote about a meeting I had with a rep from one of the brands selling this type of sharpener. He came along to show us the product in the hope that we'd sell it at the shop. When presented with the device, I took a knife from my drawer and began to drag it across a whetstone to make sure it was blunt. At which point, the rep intervened and told me not to do that as this type of sharpener isn't designed for sharpening knives that blunt. I know from years of experience that 'knives that blunt' are what most people are dealing with at home. A sharpener should be able to bring a knife back from any state, or else what's the point? And to add insult to injury, these products often retail around £160 ($208) and replacement abrasive discs at around £60 ($78). At that price you could furnish yourself with everything you need to sharpen knives and tools manually, learn a new skill *and* do a much better job.

Finally, a huge issue, which I've touched on already and applies to all of these at-home sharpening devices, is the rate at which they remove material from the knife's cutting edge. When material has not been removed from the cutting edge right up to the heel of the knife, it causes a recurve in the blade, which in turn causes frustration because it prevents the whole of the cutting edge making contact with the surface on which you're chopping or cutting. The more you sharpen the knife, the bigger the recurve gets. And the bigger the recurve, the less your cutting edge will be in contact with the chopping board, and the greater your knife-related frustrations become.

While I'm sure you can tell that I'm not a fan of home-sharpening devices, I would hate for anyone to feel chastised for having one. My primary thought when anyone tells me that they have these types of devices is, 'Well done, good work trying to keep your knives sharp.' Anyone who is going to make an effort and at least attempt to maintain their knives should feel good about it.

So, there are alternatives to whetstone sharpening for the home sharpener, but I am strongly of the opinion that by learning to sharpen by hand, on traditional whetstones, you will not only end up with superior results, you'll retain the flexibility to be able to sharpen all types of knife that come your way, however you see fit. And you'll have learned a skill that has been performed in pretty much the same way for thousands of years.

6.

## How do I know if my knife needs sharpening?

It does. If you've had your knives for some time, use them regularly, and they have never been sharpened they will definitely need it. You might think they perform okay, but the difference between a knife which just performs and a knife which properly performs is vast. A sharp knife will perfectly slice through a sheet of thin paper, while a blunt one will only cut through a carrot with the use of considerable force.

Once you've sharpened your knives and have experienced how well a properly sharpened knife performs (not how sharp they were when new, as they are rarely as sharp as they can be when new), you will then have a metric for how sharp it needs to be. When it no longer performs like this, it's time for a sharpen.

7.

## Is sharpening dangerous?

Potentially, yes. Whenever you are dealing with sharp objects there's a risk that you'll cut yourself. In fact, it's probably more accurate to say that if you regularly engage in sharpening, then there is a high chance that you'll cut yourself. I regularly get nicked while sharpening, but only superficially. So, bear these things in mind to keep yourself and others safe:

### Health and safety, best practice

— Focus on what you're doing and minimise distractions.

— If you leave the work area, put the knife down. Don't wander around with it in your hand.

— Don't place knives close to the edge of your work surface.

— Let other people know what you're doing, warn them of the dangers of distracting you unnecessarily, and ask that they warn you before they approach your work area.

— Keep cats and dogs out of your work area.

— Have a first-aid kit close to hand.

— If you do cut yourself, try to remain calm. Place whatever it is that's in your hand back on your work surface carefully and take a closer look at the damage. You'll hopefully get away with giving it a clean and popping on a plaster but if it's worse or you're at all unsure then seek medical advice.

I'll also be giving safety advice as we work through the book.

**8.**

## My knives are cheap, are they even worth sharpening?

Yes! So often people overlook sharpening their knives because they were inexpensive. The feeling is that knives need to be a certain quality to render them 'worth' sharpening. Well, this really isn't the case.

If they are the knives that you use, then they're worth sharpening. Absolutely there are better knives out there, and a better-quality knife is going to perform better and stay sharp for longer (at least it should), but only buy a new knife if you want a new knife. Buying one because your old one is blunt is wrong-headed and will only necessitate the need for another new knife further down the line.

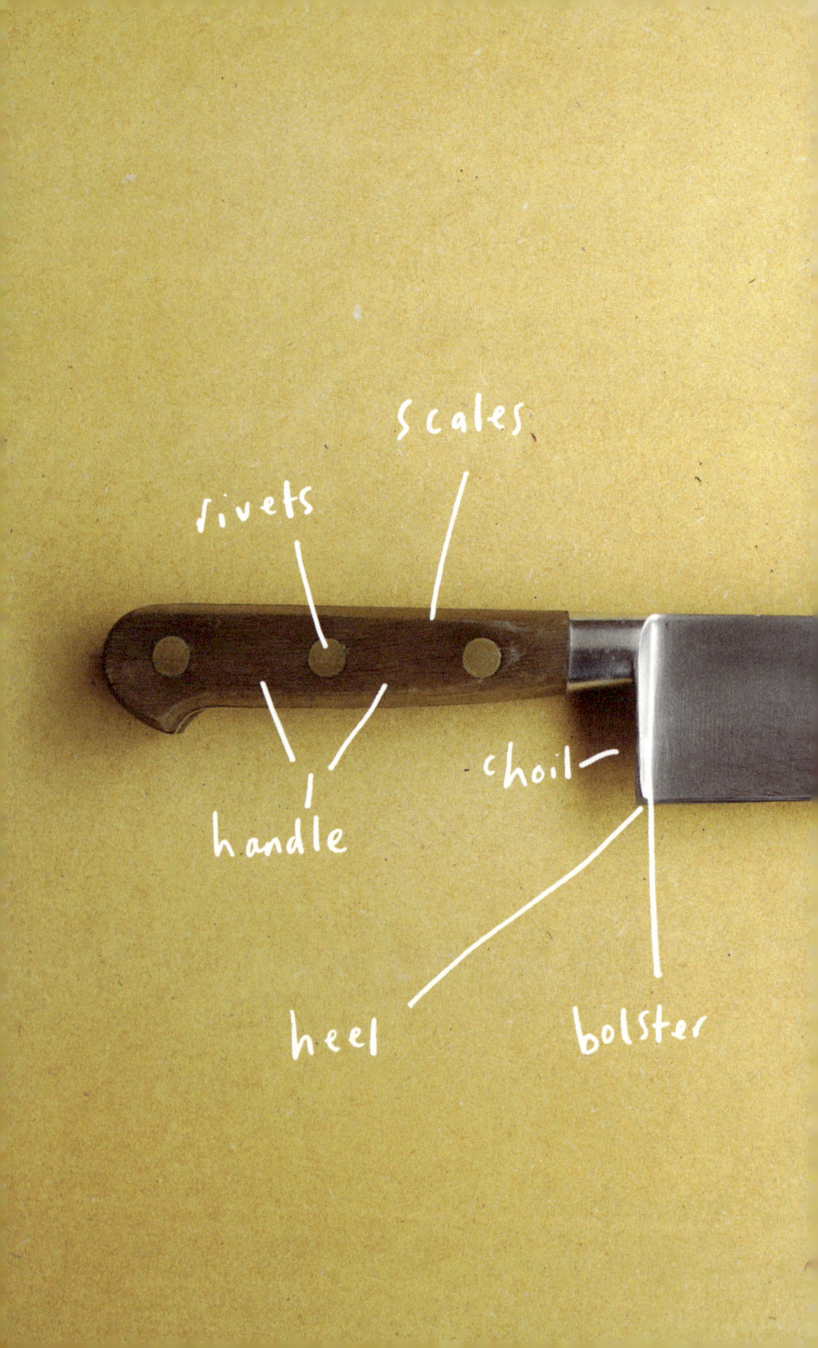
scales
rivets
choil
handle
heel
bolster

CHAPTER THREE

# The basics and the burr

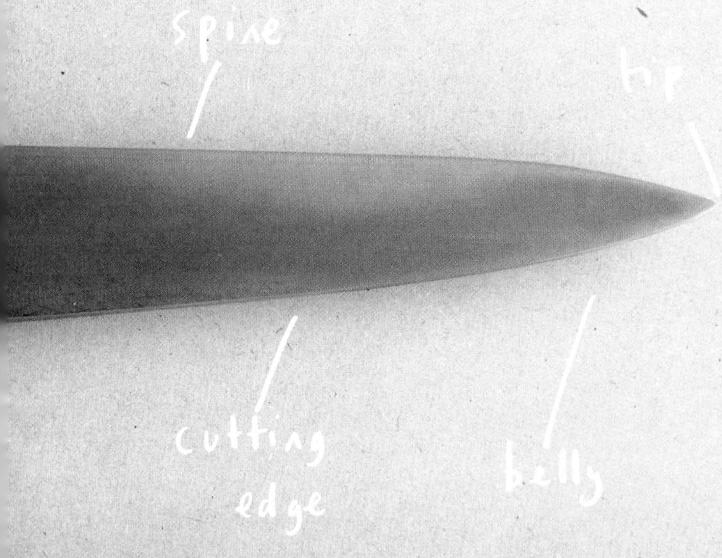

**Welcome to the theoretical part of our sharpening journey. The part that doesn't get our hands dirty but does cement our understanding of the process. The part without which we'd continue to go round in circles, only getting results occasionally and out of sheer luck.**

There's a fair bit to take in here, all of which will make more sense once you've actually begun sharpening, but stick with it and refer back as and when you need. When you consistently understand and apply these fundamental principles, it will become almost impossible not to get your knives and tools sharp.

Before we get into it, it's worth noting that out of all the tools we learn to sharpen in this book, knives are the most complex and involve the most steps. So I've chosen them as the example when covering the basics; although the technique might change from item to item (which is explained in each section), the theory of sharpening remains the same.

## Anatomy of a knife

Let's start by taking a quick look at the anatomy of a typical Western-style kitchen knife (I've chosen a Western over a Japanese-style knife as, in my experience, it's the type of knife that most people have. But if you do have Japanese knives, rest assured that almost everything here applies to your knife too, although you'll probably have a different-shaped handle). This will help to ensure you know exactly which part of the knife I'm referring to as we work through (see also Glossary of terms on page 137).

**Handle:** hopefully you know what this is, if not you must be getting through plasters at an alarming rate.

**Tang:** the extension of the blade which runs into the handle.

**Scales:** the handle material on a Western chef knife is usually sandwiched on either side of the tang (see below), where it's known as the scales.

**Rivets:** pins to help hold the scales.

**Blade:** when you hold the handle, the rest of the knife is the blade.

**Spine:** the back / topside of the blade.

**Heel:** where the blade ends and meets the bolster (or choil on a knife with no bolster).

**Choil:** the area along the back of the blade, just below the handle and where your finger rests while chopping.

**Tip:** where the blade converges with the spine to form a point.

**Apex:** where both sides of the bevel meet to form the cutting edge.

**Cutting edge:** the sharp edge that runs from tip to heel.

**Belly:** the part of the cutting edge which rounds up towards the tip. This curve differs from knife to knife.

**Bolster:** the big, chunky reinforced part of the knife between the blade and handle, traditionally used to offer some protection for the hand, reinforce the blade and centralise the balance. Can be a pain when sharpening. If not ground down occasionally it will create a recurve in the blade, preventing the edge from making full contact with the chopping board. Not present on all types of knife and notably absent from Japanese knives.

**Bevel:** angled surfaces of the knife, leading to the cutting edge.

**Primary bevel:** the part of the knife that has been ground and thinned from the thickness at the spine, tapering to the thickness behind the cutting edge. Hugely important in the functionality of the knife. The thinner the primary bevel behind the cutting edge, the better the knife will perform.

**Secondary bevel:** this makes up the sharp cutting edge. It's the part that runs off at a slightly different angle to the primary bevel, and it's the main part of the knife we're going to be working on as home sharpeners.

scale
tang
rivet
scale

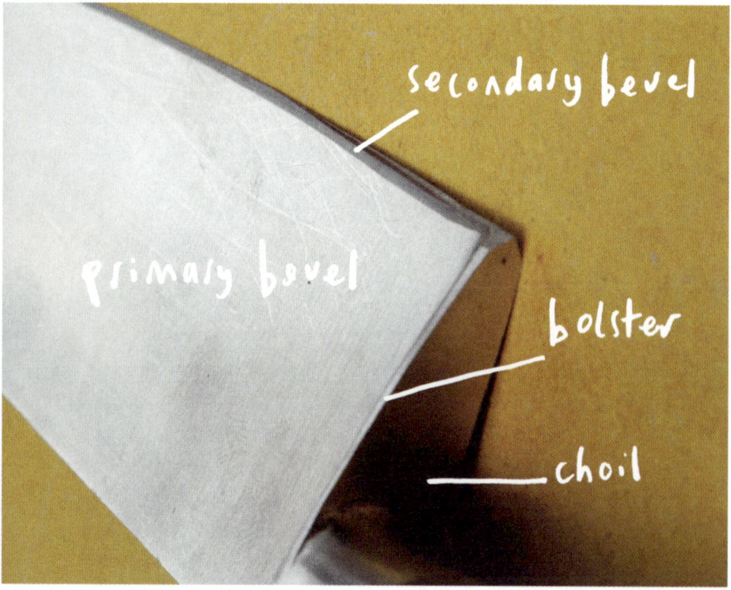
secondary bevel
primary bevel
bolster
choil

## What are we trying to achieve?

The first point we need to consider when it comes to sharpening is, 'What are we trying to do here?' We know, of course, that we're trying to sharpen our knife to enable it to perform better, but beyond that, do we know what it is we are trying to achieve at each stage of the process? Or even that there are different stages?

The first thing I like to do when teaching sharpening is to communicate to the student what this end goal looks like, to help build a clear picture of what it is we're trying to achieve when we're sharpening.



## The 3 states of the cutting edge

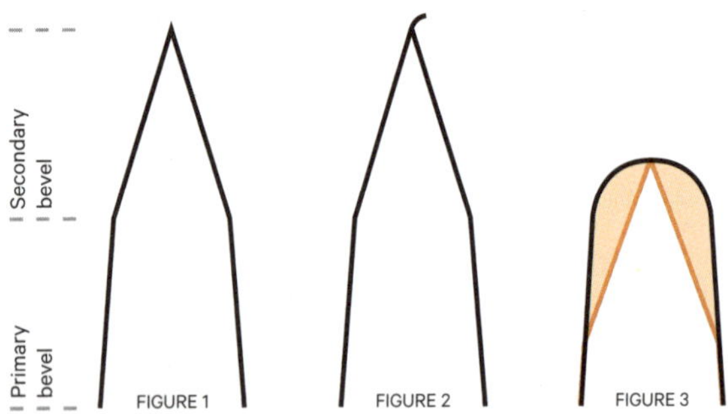


Sharp edge — Rolled edge — Blunt edge

From a quick look at Figure 1 in the diagram, we can see that both sides of the secondary bevel meet in the middle to form an apex. This apex is the cutting edge of our knife, and when it runs unbroken from the heel to the tip, we consider it to be sharp. This is how our knife should be when it's new or freshly sharpened.

We then bring this sharp knife into our kitchen and get to work on our chopping board (not a plate or our worktop!), it's a dream to use and it performs exactly as we imagine a knife should. But it won't stay that way forever. Every knife, no matter the quality, will lose its edge with use. You can expect it to take longer the better the quality, but every knife will become dull eventually. The first stage of the degradation of this edge will be the apex beginning to fold over to one side or the other—as shown in Figure 2, the 'rolled edge'. Now, at this stage, our knife is very easy to maintain; we give it a few strokes across a strop (a smooth, non-abrasive surface that we'll meet again shortly) or with a ceramic hone (a ceramic rod with a handle) and can easily push this apex back into position. This prolongs the life of our edge and avoids a more involved sharpening process.

But if we don't have a maintenance system in place, this edge continues to get knocked and bashed down until it's completely gone—just like in Figure 3 the 'blunt edge'. At which point we can consider it to be blunt. It will still function, but it's going to take increasingly more effort as the edge continues to break down, simultaneously increasing the likelihood that it will slip and cause harm.

At this stage, the knife is way beyond being able to be maintained. No amount of stropping will make it sharp again. In order to do that, we need to remove the material (imagine this as wearing off some of the steel) marked in orange on the diagram and recreate the knife's original form.

And this, my friend, is sharpening.

See over the page for my definition.

THE REUNIFICATION
OF BOTH SIDES OF
THE CUTTING EDGE
USING
MECHANICAL ACTION,
ABRASIVES
AND
PROPER TECHNIQUE

## Mechanical action

When machinery is used, the mechanical action part of sharpening may be provided by a spinning wheel or a moving belt. But for us, as we'll be sharpening by hand, the mechanical action is going to be self-powered, sorry! We're going to be moving the knife backwards and forwards across the stone ourselves.

### A note on machine sharpening

While it is possible to employ the use of machines in sharpening, it's something that requires caution. High-speed machinery can easily overheat a knife and seriously damage its ability to hold an edge. In addition to this, an inexperienced sharpener may remove much more material from the knife than required, misshaping the edge and drastically reducing the life of the knife. Unfortunately, this is how some professional sharpening services ply their trade, so investigate carefully before shipping off your prized possessions. And definitely don't try this yourself.

## Abrasives

Abrasives for sharpening can take many forms. Some people prefer to use diamond plates, some like abrasive paper systems, but the method favoured by most manual knife sharpeners is the whetstone.

A whetstone ('whet' is an old term meaning 'to sharpen', as in the phrase 'whet your appetite') is an abrasive block used for the purpose of sharpening. They vary slightly in size from maker to maker but can always be easily picked up and held in your hand. There are natural whetstones, harvested from a few specific locations around the world, but most of the whetstones used today are synthetic, made from materials such as aluminium oxide or silicon carbide.

The abrasive particles in any synthetic whetstone are produced to a specific size, bonded together and formed into a usable-sized block. A major advantage of synthetic whetstones over natural is the guaranteed consistency of this particle size.

Whetstones can be broken down into two categories: water stones and oil stones.

Oil stones are the older, more traditional type of whetstone. Here in the UK they can often be found lurking in a box in an old shed. They're made from the same types of abrasives as water stones, only with a different type of bonding agent sticking all the abrasive particles together. The main practical difference between the two is that one is lubricated with oil and the other water.

Most whetstone knife sharpeners working today, certainly the ones I know, favour water stones over oil stones, as do I. Here are a few of their advantages:

— The bonding agent used for oil stones makes them more hard-wearing but also means they're slower to remove material from a knife, as the abrasive particles aren't refreshed as quickly during use

— Using water over oil for lubrication makes cleaning up your mess easier

— Water is cheaper and easier to come by than oil

— There is greater choice when buying water stones

In addition, water stones almost always have a number on the box and the stone. This refers to the size of the particles we mentioned earlier and is known as the grit rating. Knowing the grit rating is important to us as knife sharpeners as it helps us make more educated decisions about which stones to use. In contrast, oil stones will often just be classified as coarse or medium.

## Grit ratings of whetstones

Let's have a look at grit ratings in more detail and explain what they mean on a practical level.

| 120–800 grit | 1,000–3,000 grit | 3,500 grit upwards |
|---|---|---|
| Coarse stone | Medium stone | Fine stone |

Whetstones are graded according to the size of abrasive particle they are made from and we can group them accordingly. Stones are produced at different points within each grouping, but these will vary from maker to maker. For example, within the coarse grouping, it's possible to find stones with a grit rating of 120, 150, 200, 250, 300, 400, 500, 600, 700, and 800. But rarely will any single manufacturer produce stones at all of these increments. Keep in mind:

— **The lower the number**, the larger the abrasive particle, and the faster it removes material from your knife

— **The higher the number**, the smaller the abrasive particle, and the slower it removes material from your knife

No matter where we are on this scale, a stone with any one of these grit ratings is abrasive and can remove material. So theoretically we could take a stone from the top end of the fine grouping and sharpen a blunt knife. But... it would take us a very long time indeed. Nobody has that amount of time to spend on sharpening a single knife. So, we don't use high-grit stones for sharpening. We use them for honing or refining the edge of either a sharp knife which is starting to blunt or as part of a sharpening progression, after we've finished working with a lower-grit stone.

So, when selecting stones for sharpening our initial consideration should be choosing one which is going to get the job done in a decent amount of time.

A simple way to look at it is:

- **Coarse stones:** for sharpening; they'll remove a good amount of material in a short amount of time
- **Medium stones:** take longer to remove material but can be good for restoring an edge which is in a pretty good state of repair, or for refining work done at a lower grit
- **Fine stones:** used for refining, honing or finishing the edge of a carbon steel knife

In practical terms, what does this mean to you as a home sharpener?

It's important you know about the grit scale and what the numbers on the stones mean, but my advice to you, initially at least, is to not get bogged down in all the details. You only need to start with a simple combination stone, one with a low-grit side and a medium-grit side. With this and a strop (we'll get on to this soon), you'll be able to get any knife to a state where it's sharp enough to do whatever you need it to do in the kitchen.

Common combinations are 200/1,000, 400/1,000 and 280/1,500. It doesn't matter what you go for, just as long as it's got a low/medium combination, and it's preferably not too cheap.

## A note on cheap whetstones

When you start sharpening and you begin looking for equipment to buy, you can very quickly become overwhelmed by the large number of cheap (£10–20 / $15–25), identical-looking whetstones online. I've just done a quick search and 34 of the first 40 results fit this category. As tempting as it might be to go for one of these over the more expensive options, I would encourage you not to.

While the performance certainly isn't as good as a higher-end stone, you can actually sharpen with cheap stones. They do the job, but they wear down too fast. Cheap stones are made with poor bonding agents and within a few sessions will resemble a skateboarder's half-pipe. So do yourself a favour and avoid them — you'll only be buying another one in a few months.

A few brand names to look out for when purchasing are: Naniwa, King, Shapton and Suehiro. They all produce high-quality products that I can recommend.

Now we know which stones are needed and their grit ratings, let's have a look at how we're going to use them.

# Abrasives in action

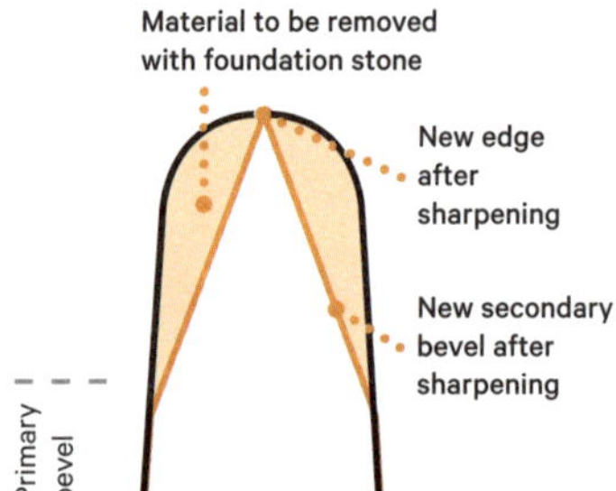


FIGURE 4

FIGURE 5

**Edge after low-grit stone**

FIGURE 6

**Edge after medium-grit stone**



## The foundation stone

When we begin to sharpen, the first stone used will always be considered the ‘foundation stone’. No matter the grit. And it’s with this foundation stone that we will remove all of the material required to reunify both sides of the cutting edge.

A quick look at Figure 4 shows us that the foundation stone does almost all of the heavy lifting when it comes to knife sharpening. We work on it until we’ve removed all the material we need (marked in orange on the diagram) to completely reunify both sides of the cutting edge, making our knife sharp enough to cut paper easily. But because the stone we have used is made from coarse, low-grit particles (enabling us to remove the material in a reasonable amount of time) we’ve been left with an edge that’s quite rough (see Figure 5). Rough enough to feel it plucking the cloth when wiping the knife, or rough enough to pull at the fibres of paper when testing.

At this point, the knife will now be sharp, because we’ve reunified both sides of the cutting edge, but as the edge is so rough and inconsistent the knife still isn’t going to perform to its full potential. But by flipping the stone over to its medium-grit side and repeating the process, we can refine our work and give ourselves a much more consistent edge. Something more akin to the edge in Figure 6. And once we've achieved this, we'll be left with a knife which is up to any job you throw at it in the kitchen.

## Hydrating your whetstone

If you're using a water stone — and most of you will be — it's going to need to be hydrated before use. Some will require a complete soak, while others only require an application of water to the stone's surface. To work out which type of stone you have, just pop it into a filled sink or bowl of water. If it starts hissing and bubbling, then you've got a soaking stone. Just leave it in there until the bubbling has stopped and it becomes fully hydrated. If you've submerged it and nothing happens then it's a sign that your stone doesn't require soaking, and you can get to work straight away!

Either way, you need to make sure the surface of the stone remains hydrated throughout the process. Once you get started, have a bowl of cold water or spray bottle to hand and apply some every now and then. The 'slurry', which appears on the surface of the stone, should be kept to a workable consistency, not stiff and dry like the bottom of the peanut butter jar (see image page 136).

## A note on flattening whetstones

During sharpening, as the knife is moving backwards and forwards across the whetstone, the abrasive particles which make up the stone get worn away. As this happens your whetstone will begin to show evidence of losing these particles and become dished. The lower the grit of the stone, the faster this will happen, but it will happen to all stones after enough use. Initially it doesn't seem like too much of an issue but eventually the stone will become so dished it's difficult to use and even more difficult to do a good job.

To keep stones in good working order, it's important that they are flattened regularly. To do this you'll need a pencil and some kind of flattening device. Your options for flattening devices are:

— **Coarse diamond plates:** good but expensive.

— **Flattening stones:** sometimes much smaller than the whetstones themselves, so can take a long time and make it difficult to get the stone properly flat. Larger versions are a good, mid-price option.

— **Low-grit Carborundum powder:** my personal favourite and the cheapest and fastest option. Can be bought online and around 500g (about 1 lb) will last a very long time. It does need to be used in conjunction with a hard, flat surface, such as a piece of marble or toughened glass.

Once you have chosen which of the above methods you're going to use to flatten your stone, start by drawing a rough 2 cm (½ in) grid across its surface in pencil. Next, making sure your stone is hydrated, take your stone flattener or diamond plate and rub it face down across the surface. This will remove a layer of stone, starting with the high spots. Make sure you apply even pressure throughout the process and liberally apply water when needed.

If using the Carborundum method, you'll be doing the same thing but in reverse; just sprinkle some powder onto your glass and rub the stone face down across it.

Keep checking the pencil markings. Eventually you'll be left with a small oval right in the middle; this is the area which sees the most action and is consequently the lowest part. Keep going until the pencil has all gone and you're left with a lovely flat stone.

A word to the wise: this is an awful job, so I'd recommend you do it regularly to avoid mammoth flattening sessions.

As you advance as a sharpener and become more comfortable, you can start to think about how your movements are wearing the stone as you work, paying attention to the corners of the stone and reducing the need for flattening. Work up to this, though, just get comfortable with the sharpening basics first.

## Proper technique

Okay, so now we've talked about mechanical action and abrasives — mostly whetstones and a bit about how to maintain them — the other key part of knife sharpening is proper technique. We get stuck into this in Chapter 4, but I do want to talk a bit about angles first.

## Angles

When it comes to sharpening knives, fear of getting the sharpening angle wrong and ruining a knife is without a doubt the single biggest concern people have — and the biggest reason people decide not to give it a try. But I'm here to tell you that it really isn't as big a deal as you think it is.

First off, what are we actually on about?

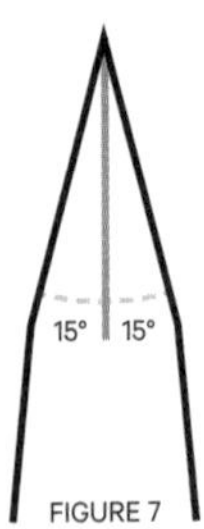

FIGURE 7

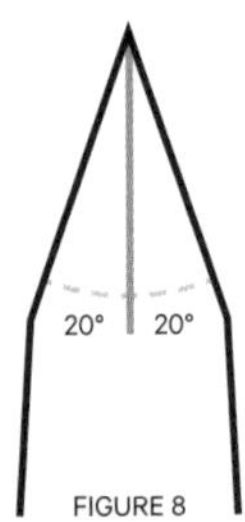

FIGURE 8

Figure 7 shows a cross-section of a knife with a bevel angle of 15 degrees. You can see that the complete angle of the bevel is actually 30 degrees, but as we only sharpen one side of the knife at a time, we only refer to the angle of one side when stating the sharpening angle of a particular knife. Figure 8 shows a knife with a bevel angle of 20 degrees (total 40 degrees). What's the difference? Well...

The edge of the knife in Figure 7 will be sharper than the knife in Figure 8.

The edge of the knife in Figure 8 will be more robust and stay sharp for longer than that of the knife in Figure 7.

So, when choosing a sharpening angle for a knife we need to strike a balance between the potential to be sharp and the potential for the knife to hold the edge we put on it.

There are many factors which affect the length of time a knife will stay sharp — the things you cut, the surfaces you cut on, how frequently you use it and the material it's made from — but the sharpening angle is a big one. There's no point in sharpening a knife to a very low angle if it's going to roll over on the first use. Your knife doesn't necessarily need to be the sharpest it could possibly be in order to do a good job.

It's generally accepted that angles with the best balance are:

— **For Western-style kitchen knives** (what most of us will have at home) – around 18–20 degrees

— **For Japanese and handmade carbon steel knives** – around 15 degrees

## So why the difference?

When knives are made, they go through a process of heat treatment. And depending on factors related to the steel and the choices made by the knife maker, a knife will end up with a certain HRC or hardness rating. Knives with a higher HRC will be able to hold an edge for longer but will be more brittle.

Of course, there are exceptions to this but, generally speaking, the Western knife-making culture has traditionally favoured a lower HRC, leading to a knife that has a slightly lower potential for sharpness and edge retention but is much less susceptible to damage like chipping. Whereas the Japanese culture has sacrificed a little durability in favour of a knife with greater potential for sharpness and edge retention.

So, coming back to our original point, we usually sharpen Japanese knives to a lower angle because they're able to retain it. We could sharpen a Western knife like this, and it would be sharper, but it wouldn't hold that edge for as long and we'd need to spend more time maintaining it.

So now you know that, when you hear people talking about the angle of the knife, what they're actually referring to is the angle of the bevel or, more specifically, one side of the bevel, as we only sharpen one side at a time.

But rest assured that by getting your angle a few degrees out from the recommended range you are not going to damage your knife. It will still be better than it was before! A knife is way better if maintained at slightly the 'wrong' angle than if it's neglected out of a fear of ruining it. Just get it sharp! What's more important is that you are consistent with the angle you choose.

So when sharpening, the more we raise the spine of the knife from the stone, the higher the angle of the bevel we'll end up putting on the knife. And the closer the spine is to the whetstone, the lower the angle of the bevel will end up being. Make sense?

So, how do we find the 'correct' angle? Well, we'll get to that on page 68, and what I'm not going to do is recommend you use an angle guide. In my opinion, this is a sure-fire way to ensure you don't progress as a sharpener. Better to make a few mistakes now and learn how to do it properly.

Feeling confident with this is one of the trickier parts of the sharpening process. It's not hard but it is going to take a bit of practice to build up the muscle memory. Once you've got that you'll be off to the races and will rarely think of it again! So, now you know a bit of the theory behind angles, we'll go into more detail about how to do it for each particular item in the chapters that follow.

## Raising the burr

This is the big one—you're now looking at the most important word in sharpening:

**BURR**

When we begin to remove material with our whetstone (or file if we're sharpening a tool, but we'll come on to this) our aim, as we've already covered, is to reunify both sides of our cutting edge and create a new apex. And luckily for us, we're going to be given a very clear and definitive sign once this has been achieved.

As we remove material from one side of the bevel and then the other, we will gradually bring them closer together, working away until they've eventually been reunified, and a new apex created. We likely won't be able to tell this by looking at it with the naked eye, but what we will be able to do is feel it with our finger. And this thing we can feel is called the burr.

If we don't remove enough material to raise the burr, we don't remove enough material to reunify both sides of the cutting edge, create a new apex and get a sharp knife. It's as simple as that.

This burr is created at the moment we've removed enough material to reunify both sides of the edge into a new apex. Once we have this and then continue to move the knife back and forth across the abrasive, we'll begin to push some material over this new apex. It hangs and slightly folds over, rather than being worn away like the material lower down the bevel.

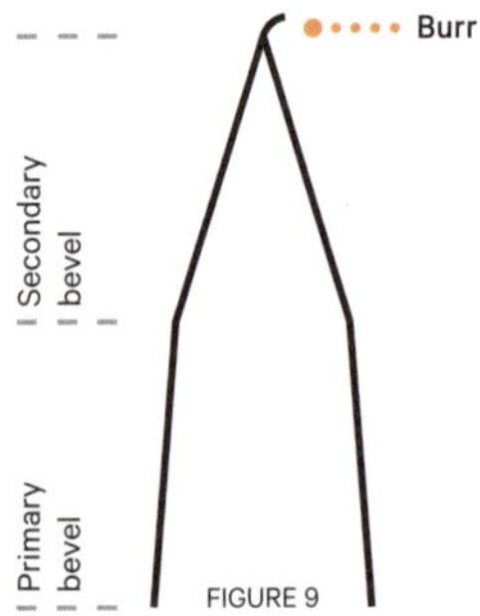


FIGURE 9

Raising the burr

Raising and identifying the burr is going to be the thing we look for to tell us our knife is sharp. And we'll aim to raise and remove it on every stone as we progress. This will involve the removal of a much larger amount of material when working on our foundation stone, after which we'll just be removing a very thin layer, enough to refine the scratch pattern left by the previous stone and improve the consistency of our new edge.

Once raised, the burr will always be on the opposite side to the side you last sharpened. If at some point you notice the burr is partly on one side and partly on the other, it's not an issue, it just shows that you last removed material from different sides of the knife in different places. Trust me, this will all make sense when you start sharpening.

## Stropping

In the final part of our basics chapter, we're going to look at stropping. When I mention stropping to people, the first image it usually conjures up is that of a barber in a western movie, passing their cut-throat razor backwards and forwards across a leather strap in a slightly intimidating fashion. If that's what you thought then you'd be right, this is exactly what we're talking about! Except strops for knives are better without the flex, so they're usually a piece of leather attached to a piece of wood to give it a hard back.

A strop is a soft, flat, non-abrasive surface over which the bevel of a knife is passed back and forth to clean up and fully align its edge (see image page 59).

We use the strops at the final stage of our sharpening process. It adds the finishing touches to the work done on the whetstones and helps our knife to perform to the best of its ability.

Traditionally the stropping medium would be leather, but vinyl, denim, cardboard, cork, newspaper, and even balsa wood, are all good alternatives.

As well as being used at the end of the sharpening process, stropping is also the method we recommend for maintaining your knives on a regular basis. Just pass them over your strop (using the method described in the next chapter) before every use and you'll keep that edge sharp for a much longer time—reducing the time and effort you need to spend sharpening.

## How to make a strop

Strops are available to buy from plenty of places online and they aren't expensive. They're a simple product, usually made by gluing a piece of leather or vinyl to a piece of wood. If you happen to have some of these materials lying around at home then making one yourself is always an option. Here's how:

### What you will need

— **A piece of wood**, something that isn't going to warp. I use 18 mm (11⁄16 in) plywood, approx. 200 × 70 mm (8 × 3 in)
— **Some strong adhesive**, I use Evo-Stik flooring adhesive
— **A piece of thick leather or vinyl** (linoleum), slightly bigger than your piece of wood

### Method

Evenly coat the back of your leather or vinyl with glue and stick it to your wood. Make sure there are no bubbles and leave it somewhere to dry, popping a few books on top to keep it flat. Once dry, trim the edge of your stropping material down to the size of the wood and away you go.

You may be aware that there are stropping compounds available. This is a spray or a paste that can be applied to a strop to introduce a fine abrasive to its surface. While these can be helpful, particularly when sharpening carbon steel knives, they aren't by any means essential. Personally, I don't bother with them on my home strops.

Using a strop

## A note on geometrical sharpness

Have you had the experience of using a knife on something like a carrot or a parsnip, and you can hear the veg cracking? This happens when the sharp knife slices the flesh and begins to cut your carrot, but at a certain point, if the knife is too thick behind the cutting edge, it begins to wedge the carrot and split it (much like an axe would), rather than cutting it in two.

One of the reasons higher-end knives often perform so much better is because they have been ground thinly, enabling the cutting edge to stay in contact with the food through the entirety of the cut. Removing material and improving the geometry of a knife is a time-consuming and therefore costly process, hence why it is often associated with higher-end knives.

Even if your knife is relatively thin behind the cutting edge when it's new, over time you sharpen your knife and remove material, pushing its edge further and further into the thicker material, affecting the geometry and how it performs.

During the whetstone sharpening process, the sharpener is fully in tune with their activities, regularly checking their work and making decisions about how to progress. This fastidious assessment allows the knife to be sharpened while removing the least amount of material necessary, prolonging the life of the knife and preserving the valuable edge geometry.

Inevitably, after a certain amount of use, the knife will begin to perform differently — it's unavoidable. From my experience it seems that most day-to-day knife users don't seem too bothered by this, but for those who are, and those looking to preserve the functionality of higher-priced or precious knives, it is possible to put them through a process called thinning. Thinning is when material is removed from the primary bevel with a coarse whetstone or a grinding machine until the sharpener is happy with the new geometry. This is a slow process and can therefore be expensive, but it can make a huge difference to how your knife performs.

It is an advanced technique, so not one we will be covering in this book. If you have a knife that you feel needs thinning, my advice would be to seek out your local whetstone sharpener and send it along to them. They'll do a better job and it will be much easier than doing it yourself.

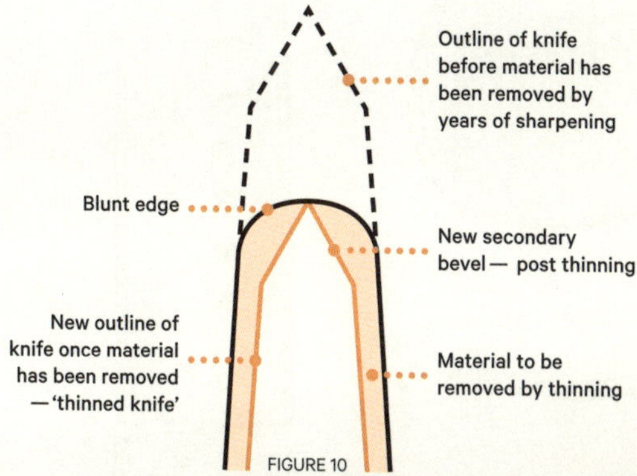


FIGURE 10

Material removed by thinning process

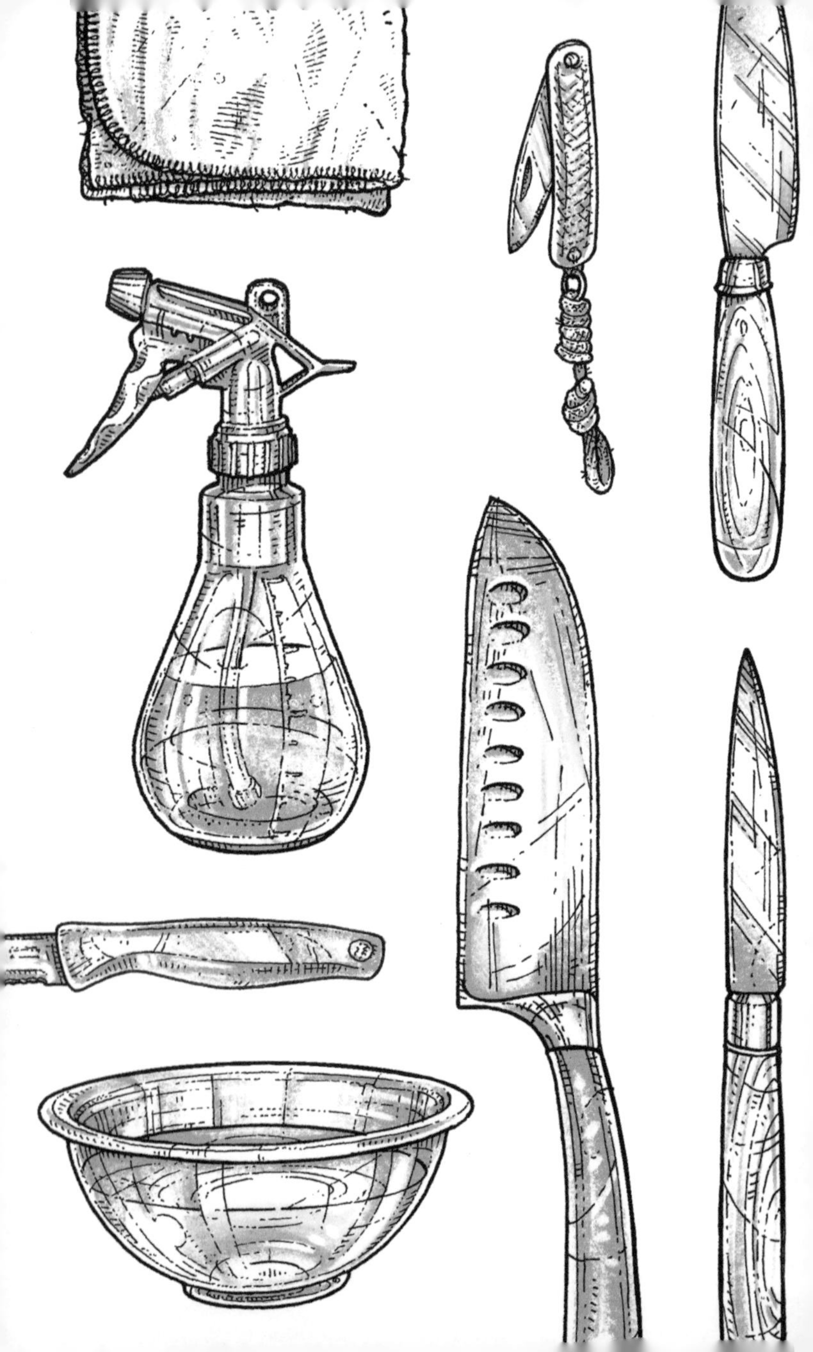

CHAPTER FOUR

# How to sharpen a knife

**Okay, it's the bit we've been building up to. It's time to finally learn how to sharpen your knives, so let's get into it.**

In this section I'll describe the steps required in detail to help you gain a full understanding of the process. I suggest you read it straight through once, and then follow along again as you're sharpening. In Chapter 8 you'll find quick reference guides. These are intended to help remind you of the steps once you understand what it is you're supposed to be doing.

### What you will need

- **Coarse and medium-grit whetstones** or a back-to-back combination stone
- **A strop**
- **Water in a sink or bowl** big enough to fit the whetstones
- **Water in a spray bottle**
- **A couple of cloths,** kitchen tea towels work just fine
- **A stable workspace to sharpen your knife on,** a kitchen worktop is ideal

STEP 1

## Assess the knife

Take a good look at your knife and assess whether it is blunt or just needs a light sharpen? Is it damaged — is the edge chipped, or the tip missing?

I think it would be fair to assume that most of the knives being sharpened off the back of this book will fall into the blunt category, even if you don't think it performs too badly. So, unless it has been sharpened at some point over the last six months, it will almost certainly benefit from a low-grit foundation stone.

If your knife is damaged, carry on reading for now — there's a section for that at the end of this chapter.

STEP 2

## Choose and prepare your stone

Cast your mind back to Chapter 3 when we talked about the first stone in our progression being our foundation stone: well, this is that. For most of us, this will likely be a coarse stone: 250–400 would be ideal.

Assuming it's not an oil stone, hydrate your whetstone in the bowl of water until the bubbles stop.

Place the whetstone in a stone holder if you have one (sometimes the stone comes in a case that doubles as a holder), or simply place the stone on a damp cloth on the work surface. The holder just needs to prevent the stone from slipping around. Ensure it's flat or flatten according to instructions on page 50–51.

STEP 3

## The correct hand position

Take the knife in your dominant hand and place the heel (if you need a reminder, see 'Anatomy of a knife' on page 34) in the bottom corner of the stone: right if you're right-handed, left if you're left-handed.

Have the cutting edge facing towards you and running at an angle of around 45 degrees from the bottom corner.

Place the thumb of the hand holding the knife at the heel, as close to the edge as you can without it hanging over and touching the stone.

Place the index and middle fingers of the opposite hand on the upward-facing bevel. They should be touching the thumb and as close as they can be towards the edge without touching the stone.

Try to use the boney points of your fingers to focus the pressure if you can; we're aiming to press down through the knife and remove material from the area underneath these fingers only.

We're going to break down the whole knife into two-finger chunks, moving them up in sections, as seen in the images opposite.

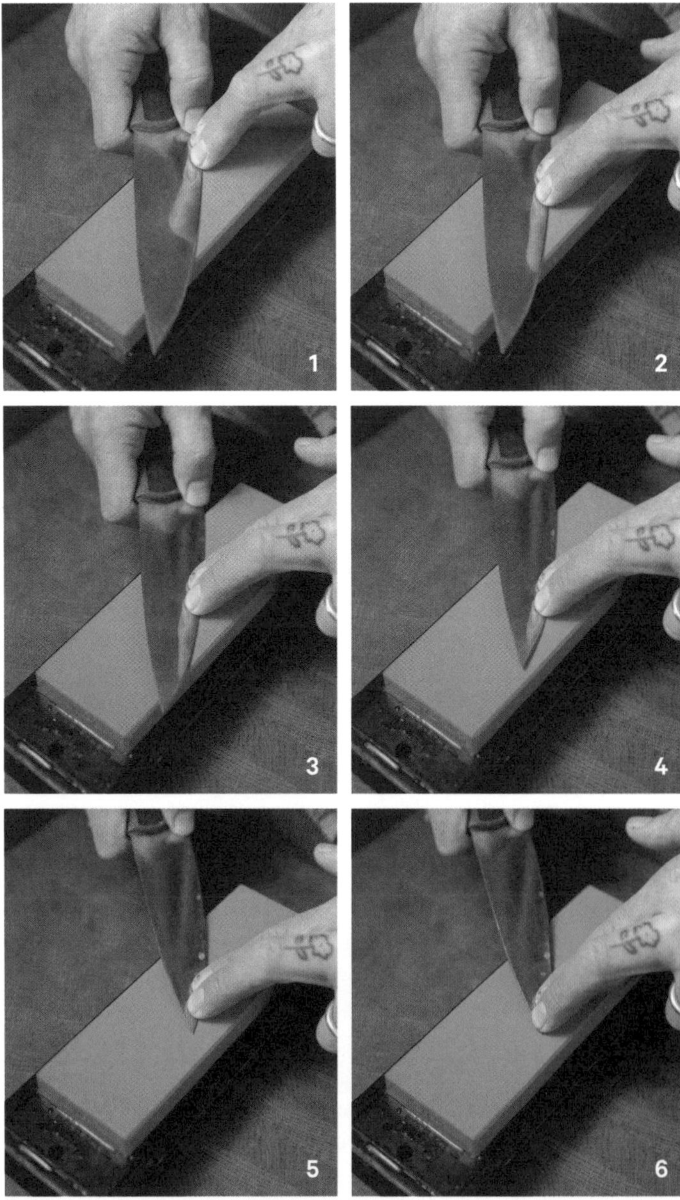
1
2
3
4
5
6

## STEP 4

# Finding the angle

To familiarise ourselves with the sharpening angle, we're going to experiment by eliminating angles that are definitely wrong.

Starting with the knife and your fingers in the correct position, swivel the spine up towards the ceiling (1). We know for sure that this angle is wrong. All we would do if we started sharpening like this is to flatten off the edge.

Next, with fingers still in position, we're going to take the angle down to the opposite extreme, so the side of the knife is laid flat on the stone (2). This is also obviously wrong—all we'd do here would be to scratch the side of the knife while the secondary bevel (see page 38) was out of contact with the stone.

Again, we're going to move the spine back towards the ceiling but not as far as before, then back down again, but not so much that it's touching the stone (3) and (4).

Keep doing this, gradually reducing the extent to which you raise or lower the spine until you feel that you've got the right angle (5) and (6). Sharpening is a lot about feel, and there will come a time when you can easily feel that you've come to rest nicely on the bevel.

But as a new sharpener, with all of these steps running through your head, it can be tricky to tune into this feeling straight away (at least until you've got a few hours practice under your belt). So for now, we're going to need to rely upon a different method to get you started.

I recommend placing the back of your forefinger (or little finger if you have huge hands, thumb if you have small hands) on the stone with the very tip of your finger under the spine of the knife (see page 70). This is a great

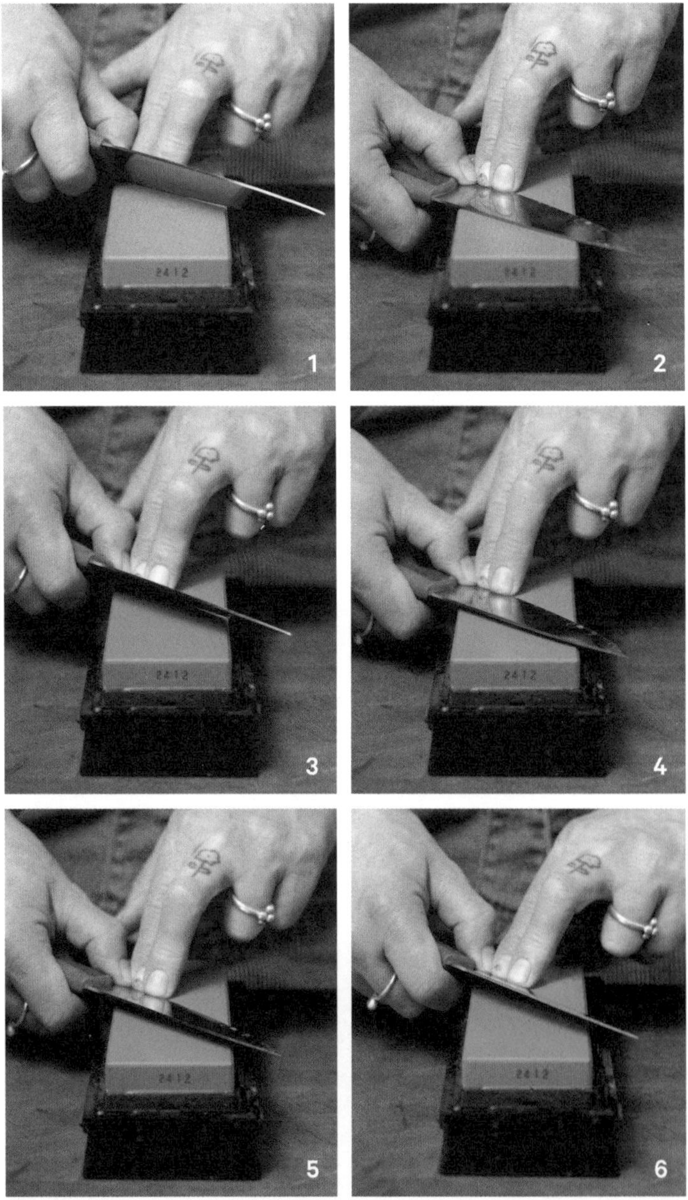
1
2
3
4
5
6

way to approximate the required angle and a reliable way to check for consistency throughout the process. Just place your finger back on the stone every now and then and adjust the angle if needed. You'll be able to tell if you've been inconsistent by looking at your bevel: if it is bigger in some places than others, you'll know your angle has changed. You're aiming for the same-sized bevel along the whole edge.

Using finger to find the sharpening angle

## A note on pressure

When sharpening, the amount of pressure you use is a great tool and should be used to your advantage. It can be varied throughout the process: more pressure to remove more material at a faster rate; less pressure to refine edges and remove material more slowly.

If you find that raising the burr on your low-grit stone is taking a really long time, it might be that you just need to apply more pressure.

This can only really be fully understood by experimentation. Play with it as you go along, and you'll quickly work out how much pressure to apply and when. Just take care that you're never using so much pressure that it's a struggle to move the knife across the stone, as that would be too much!



**STEP 5**

# Removing material

Now that we're happy with our angle, it's time to start removing material. So, with pressure at the heel from our thumb and from our fingers on the bevel, we want to start making strokes.

A stroke is the journey backwards and forwards, from the bottom of the whetstone to the top and back down again. We want to make full use of the effort we're putting in and remove material in both directions, not just one way or the other.

We're going to make 6 strokes in our initial finger position, before moving them up the knife to the next position and repeating. Do this until you reach the tip of the knife.

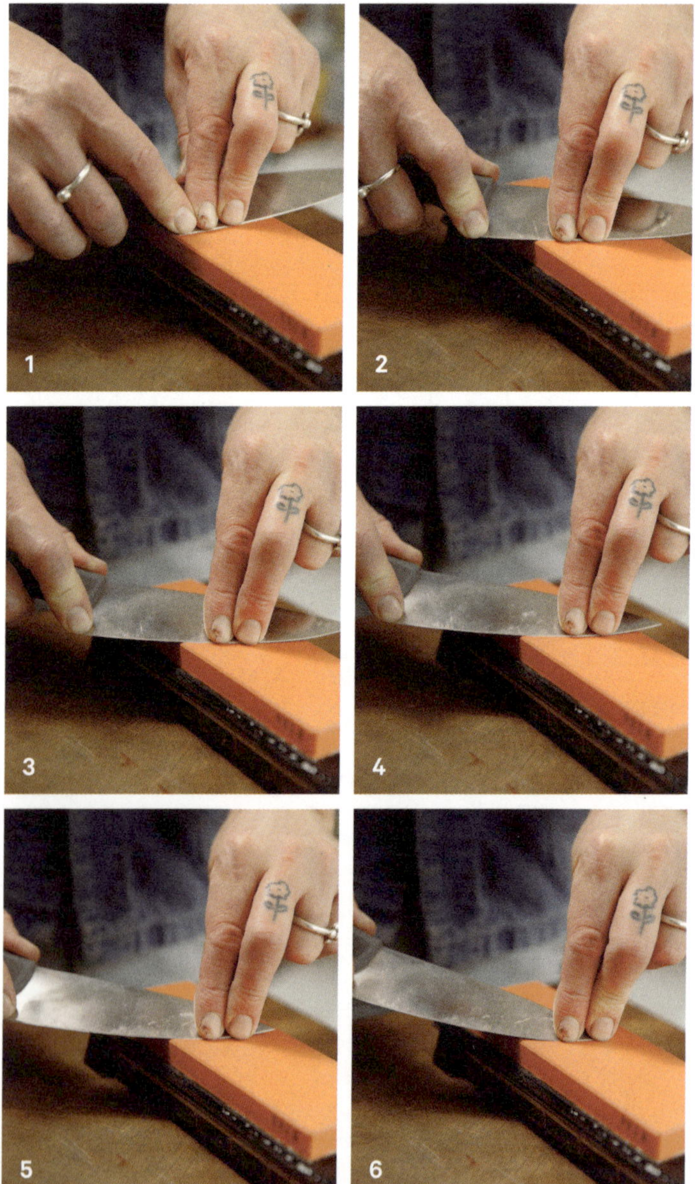
1
2
3
4
5
6

Note that once you pass the belly of the knife, due to its curvature, the bevel will likely be off the stone, at which point I recommend the following: keeping your wrist firm, move your elbow out and up slightly until the bevel comes back into contact with the stone. Experiment with this until you are confident you're removing material from the entire bevel, right up to the tip.

Top tip: when the tip of your knife is in contact with the stone it will leave a thin line, just like a pencil has drawn on the stone. You need to see this to ensure you're sharpening right up to the tip.

Great work, you've now completed one full pass on the first side of your knife.

Next, you want to flip the knife over so the cutting edge is facing away from you (pictured opposite).

The forefinger of your dominant hand will now replace the thumb and apply downward pressure at the heel. Both thumbs rest on the spine and the first two fingers of your non-dominant hand will reach over the blade and onto the upper side of the secondary bevel, just like before, so they can apply direct pressure to the area where you will be sharpening.

Now find your angle again. Experiment by moving the spine up and down until you feel the bevel like before, or use your fingertip under the spine to set the angle.

Begin to make strokes, counting six in each position, making sure to apply pressure from the fingers while incrementally moving them along the blade.

This time, when you've passed the belly, to ensure the bevel makes full contact with the stone right up the tip, you're going to want to bring your elbow into the body and up a little, until you see that fine line on the stone again.

Now you've made a full pass on each side, do it again. We want to do 2 full passes on each side — with 1 pass being another 6 strokes (remember 1 stroke is the journey from the bottom of the whetstone to the top and back down again) — before stopping to inspect your work.

Firstly, have a good look at the bevel, as it's going to tell you everything you need to know about how you've been getting on. A few questions to ask yourself:

— Is the bevel the same size the whole way along the knife? If not, your angle has been inconsistent.

— Are there scratches up the side of the knife? If so, your angle has become too low.

— Is there a definite bevel or does it seem to round in towards the side of the knife? If so, the angle has likely been moving up and down during the stroke and you've failed to create a defined bevel.

— Is the bevel present all the way to the tip and the heel? If not, try lifting your handle a little higher to ensure contact right to the tip or apply more pressure at the heel.

— Is the bevel very faint? More pressure is required.

All of these problems can be addressed by ensuring your wrist is steady and firm, checking your angle before you start, and again halfway through the process. And ensuring you adapt your position to make full contact with the bevel, right up to the tip.

STEP 6

## Checking for the burr

Once we've checked our bevel, we also need to assess how we're progressing towards reunifying both sides of the cutting edge and getting our knife sharp again. And to do that we're going to check for — say it together — the burr!

Holding the knife in your non-dominant hand with the edge facing towards your dominant hand, place the pads of your first two fingers on the primary bevel of the knife — the side opposite to the side you last worked on. Now, slowly and carefully move your fingers out and over the side of the secondary bevel. If you have raised a burr you should feel it scratching your fingers at this point.

If you don't feel it straight away, then try a few more times. Tuning in to feeling the burr is often one of the trickiest parts for new sharpeners. You can also try moving your thumbnail very slowly over the secondary bevel; you should feel it catch on the burr as it goes over the edge.

Have you got a burr all the way along the knife? If you don't feel the burr at all then go back to the stone and keep repeating the instructions in Step 5 until you find it. Remember, there is no right or wrong amount of passes it should take to find the burr. All that matters is that you find it, so keep going until you do. If you've been working for a long time then you probably need more pressure, so try pressing a little harder on the next pass.

If you've only raised a burr in a small section of the knife, then I recommend carrying out another two passes before checking again.

If you've got a burr in a large section of the knife but are only missing it in one or two small sections then it's fine to go back to the stones and carry out a pass again in those sections only (but always on both sides, remember) until you've raised a burr the whole way along the knife.

Remember that raising the burr is the most fundamental aspect of sharpening and without it you will not get a sharp knife, so keep going until you've got it!

Checking for the burr

STEP 7

## Removing the burr

So now you've raised a burr, you've already done most of the work towards sharpening your knife.

The next stage is to remove the burr. The burr has shown us that we've reunified both sides of the knife, but now it's got to go! We don't want it interfering with the work we're doing at the next stage.

Back to the same position as before. Repeat the process again with everything exactly the same but with much, *much* less pressure and at half the speed you were moving the knife before.

The aim here is to move the bevel lightly across the surface of the stone and wear down as much of the burr as possible, while minimising the amount of new burr formed on the other side of the knife.

Repeat the process until you've done 2 passes on each side.

Now check your progress by feeling for the burr again on each side. You don't want to be able to feel it at all, so if you can still feel it, go back to the stones and repeat. If it's being really stubborn then experiment with pressure and stroke length — sometimes you might need a little more pressure, sometimes less, but it will always need to be a lot less than when you originally created the burr. If there is a particularly stubborn spot then adjust your stroke length to very small, 2 cm (¾ in) long strokes and (I know this sounds strange) lean into the stone and focus your attention on the areas in question. This increased awareness will allow you to really tune into what's going on and better tailor your actions to the job that needs doing.

STEP 8

## Edge trailing

Once all the burr is removed, we can now carry out some edge-trailing strokes to finish off the work on our foundation stone. This isn't a new technique, just a new term for half of the technique we've been using up to now. And we do it to nicely align the edge and clean it up before we progress to the next stone.

When the knife is moving away from us as in the image, the cutting edge is trailing the movement, but when we pull it back to us, it's leading the movement.

We want to eliminate the edge-leading strokes.

So, we need to push the knife to the top of the stone in the direction of the arrow (pictured), lift it straight up without rolling the knife or dropping it off the edge, and return it to the starting position. Repeat this for 3 edge-trailing strokes in each finger position before flipping the knife over and repeating on the second side of the knife—only this time you'll be starting from the top of the stone and bringing the knife towards you.

Once we've done 2 passes on each side, we consider the foundations of a sharp knife well and truly laid—well done!

Making an edge-trailing stroke

HOW TO SHARPEN A KNIFE

## STEP 9

# Successive stones

Okay, so we've reunified both sides of the bevel and sharpened the knife with our foundation stone. Now we're going to be refining the new edge so it's time to switch to our medium-grit stone, 1,000–1,500 would be ideal. And luckily for you, there is nothing new to learn here, you just need to repeat steps 2–7 exactly as you did on the first stone.

A couple of things to keep in mind. It's important that you raise a burr again here. That's going to let you know that you've removed a layer of material from the bevel, and refined the scratch pattern left by the coarse-grit stone.

But you already removed the lion's share of the material when you reunified the sides of the cutting edge on the first stone, so raising a burr again shouldn't take anywhere near as long. If it's taking a long time, you might have lowered your angle slightly, so keep an eye on this.

The grit size in your medium stone is much smaller than that of the coarse stone, so the burr will always be smaller and consequently more difficult to find. It might be necessary to use your nails to find it rather than relying on the pad of your fingers.

It's important to learn to feel the burr by hand. It won't take much practice, but it will take some. If you're having issues, experiment using your thumb instead of your fingers. Another thing you can do to check the work you've done on the medium-grit stone is to look carefully along the bevel. You shouldn't see any coarse scratches from the lower-grit stone. There should be a consistent, more polished finish along the whole bevel. Problem areas will likely be the tip and heel, so pay special attention to these.

If you're sharpening a carbon steel knife and you have a high-grit stone, you can use it now to refine the edge further, repeating the process again before moving on to stropping.

STEP 10

## Stropping

Once you've repeated all the steps and are happy with the edge, you're ready to strop. Stropping is going to put the finishing touches to your work. You've removed the material to reunify both sides of the bevel with your foundation stone, you've made your edge more consistent with your medium-grit stone and now, with your strop, you're going to properly align the apex. Just a few passes is going to bring together all your efforts and make the knife sing!

On your strop, you're going to be using only edge-trailing strokes (edge-leading would cut your stropping medium) but only 1 in each finger position this time, instead of 6. Then repeat on alternating sides about 5 times. This is what's going to really make it perform well.

Make sure you get right up to the tip and down to the heel. If you miss any sections, it's likely that your knife won't perform to its fullest potential in that area.

And if you've raised and removed the burr properly, but your knife still isn't performing as you'd hoped, then strop it again. Its powers cannot be overestimated!

That's all our practical work done now! You should have yourself a lovely sharp knife—and the beginnings of the confidence to become a competent home sharpener.

As you will probably have picked up, knife sharpening is a lot about feel. Practise as much as you can, as then it will become more intuitive. Muscle memory will build up and you'll need to rely less on these instructions, and more on your own observations about what's going on.

Please don't worry about ruining your knives. The chances of you doing something irreparable are almost zero. But, that being said, we don't recommend you start on your fanciest knife if you have one!

## A note on maintaining your new edge

Now your knife is in the shape of its life, it's really easy to maintain it. Just have your strop close to hand in the kitchen and make 5 alternating passes of edge-trailing strokes before each use. This will correct the apex after its last use and put your knife right back to being sharp again.

But remember, your strop isn't abrasive, so it's not going to remove material or work to maintain your knife once it's lost its edge. When stropping no longer feels effective, it's time to sharpen again.

## A note on repairs

At the start of this chapter, I mentioned that you should assess your knife for damage before you begin to sharpen. As this is a beginners' book, we aren't going to go into much detail about repairing damaged knives, but it would be remiss to leave it out completely.

If you discover your knife has a chip, it can still be sharpened as is, although it obviously isn't going to perform to the best of its ability.

To get the chip out, raise your sharpening angle a lot, to around 60 degrees, and work across your stone until you've passed the chip. Then you can return to your normal angle and begin sharpening. You should note that material will need to be removed from the entire edge like this. If you just remove extra material from the chipped area, you'll end up with a misshapen edge.

Missing tips can be repaired in much the same way, although we recommend you consider taking most of the material from the spine if possible. It's better to slightly alter the shape of the spine than to round out the tip and push up the edge into much thicker material. Try to blend in your work by removing material from further back along the spine as well, not just at the very tip.

Recurves at the heel — caused by uneven removal of material in the past — can be repaired by grinding the heel and/or bolster of your knife at 90 degrees across your stone until the edge is straight again.

Always stick to your lowest-grit stone when carrying out this work and try to work on the corners to spread the wear. Remember to refine the work done on bolsters and spines with your higher-grit stones later. Sharp corners and rough spines can be particularly unpleasant to the touch.

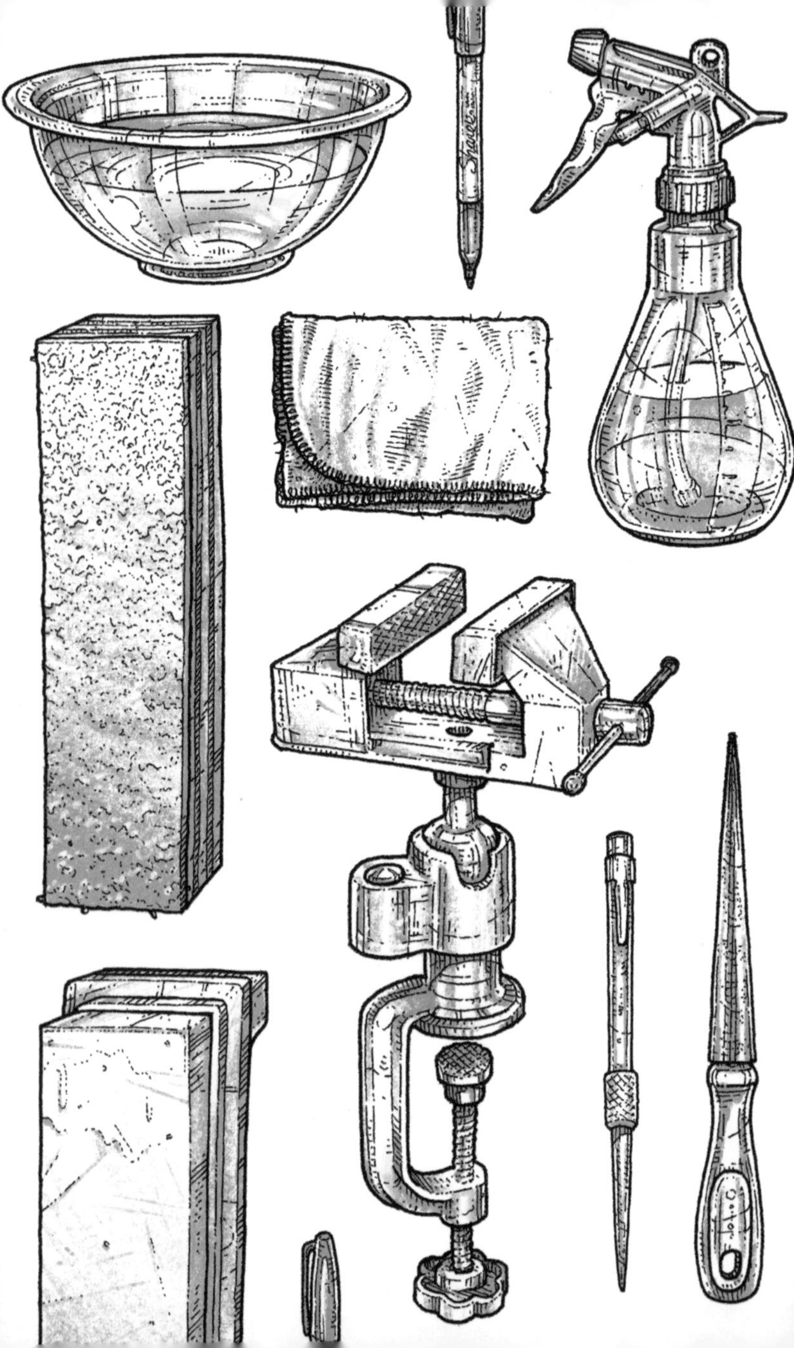

CHAPTER FIVE

# How to sharpen serrated knives

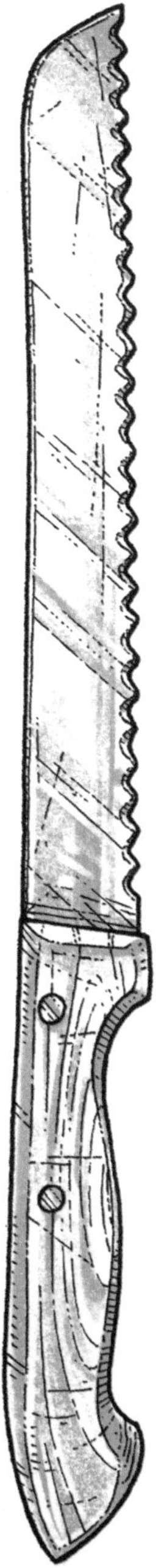

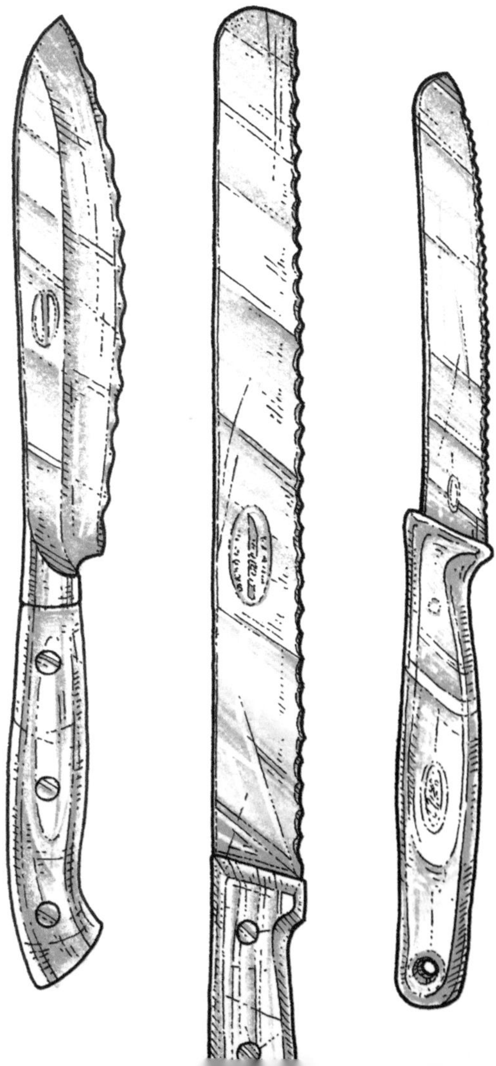

**It's a common assumption that bread knives can't be sharpened, but not only can they be sharpened, they can be sharpened at home, by you, with relative ease!**

When we're talking about serrated knives, we're usually talking about bread knives, although serrated knives can also include steak knives, serrated utility or tomato knives, even some patisserie knives. Rather than having a straight edge running from heel to tip, which performs its action when pushed through food, the edge of a serrated knife is broken up with scallops or serrations (going forward, I'll just refer to them as scallops for ease) and performs more like a saw, when pushed backwards and forwards across food.

The theory behind sharpening a serrated knife is no different to sharpening a straight-edged knife. We're just trying to reunify the bevel inside the scallop with the back of the knife, technically making it a single-bevel knife and increasing its potential for sharpness.

As a serrated knife is used, the apex between the flat back and the scalloped bevel gets rolled and flattened out. But as these bevels are tucked away in tiny troughs, you can't just work the knife across a whetstone or pull it through a home sharpening device, as you'll destroy the peaks and ruin the knife's saw-like function.

Instead we need to distil our abrasive down into something small enough to fit comfortably between the serrations without distorting their shape. For this, I recommend a conical diamond file, much like the two types shown on page 90. Best to get hold of both the conical and retractable types, as some serrated knives will suit one, and some will suit the other.

**What you will need**

- **Conical diamond file**
- **Retractable diamond file**
- **Vice,** a small articulated one is best, although you can make do with a table vice if you already have one
- **Marker pen**
- **Medium-grit whetstone**
- **A strop**
- **Water in a sink or bowl** big enough to fit the stones in
- **Water in a spray bottle**
- **A couple of cloths**
- **A solid place to sharpen on,** a kitchen worktop is ideal



### STEP 1

## Preparing to sharpen

Clamp the spine of your knife in the vice, about halfway up the blade, making sure that you've clamped enough material so it won't ping out as soon as you start working. Now take a marker pen and colour in the bevel inside the scallops. Make sure you get right up to the edges as this is going to help with our angle finding (see image overleaf).

Using a marker pen to find the correct sharpening angle

STEP 2

## Finding the angles

Take a good look at the bevels. It's at this stage we need to make a decision about our sharpening angle. Ideally, we will work the whole bevel, being faithful to the original angle, removing material from its entire face until we've reunified the scalloped bevel with the back of the knife.

Sometimes, in my experience, if the bevel is very low, it can be difficult to stay true to the original bevel angle without affecting the shape of the scallops. In which case, I recommend the addition of a micro-bevel along the cutting edge. This is essentially a very small bevel on a larger bevel, usually used to reinforce the cutting edge but a good option here to ensure you don't affect the shape of the scallops.

STEP 3

## Sharpening

Take your diamond file—whichever one best fits into the scallops of the knife you're sharpening—and carefully work backwards and forwards inside the first scallop. If you're working across the whole scallop you should see that you're removing all the pen markings from the front to the back. If you're doing this with each stroke your angle is correct.

If you're just working a micro-bevel, you want to see that you're removing a crescent moon-like amount from the cutting edge of the scallop.

Whichever method you're using, you want to keep removing material until you raise a burr across the back of

Choosing the best file for the job

the entire scallop, from the top of the scallop on the right, to the top of the scallop on the left.

Once you're sure of that, you can now move on to the next scallop and then the next, ensuring you work consistently along the entire length of the knife.

By the time you reach the end you will have reunified both sides of the cutting edge and created a new apex. Now, take your knife out of the vice. It's time to remove the burr you've created across the back of the knife.

STEP 4

## Removing the burr

Again, there are two options, both of which require a soaked whetstone.

In option 1, we again remain faithful to the knife and place the back—opposite side to the scallops—completely flat on the medium-grit whetstone, at the end furthest away from you.

Apply pressure to the upper side of the serrations above where you've raised the burr, and make an edge-leading stroke. When you reach the bottom of the stone, lift the knife, replace it back to where you began the stroke, and repeat. Work your way along the knife and continue to do this until the burr has been completely worn away. We don't use edge-trailing strokes here as we're trying to avoid pushing the burr over, where it will end up hiding between the serrations, making it trickier to remove.

This is the best way of being completely faithful to the original grind of your knife. But if you elect to use this method, the major downside is that you'll be left with lots of scratches on the back—less than ideal and arguably worse than slightly altering the back of your knife, which we'll do if we choose the second option.

Here we're going to do pretty much everything as we did in option 1, but we're going to raise the spine of the knife off the stone, not much, about 5 degrees. By doing this and applying a decent amount of pressure to the knife, above the burr, we'll wear it down like we did in option 1, but we'll avoid making the scratches. The downside is that we'll alter the look of the back of the knife slightly, as we'll have created a bevel that wasn't there before. This isn't a bad thing necessarily. Slightly thinning the edge like this could improve performance, but you also risk wearing down the peaks between the scallops, so keep that angle nice and low!



**STEP 5**

## Strop

Carefully make 3 passes of edge-trailing strokes over each side of your knife on the strop, alternating between the flat back and the scalloped front. I recommend using the long edge of your strop so you can properly get into the scallops. Make an edge-trailing stroke between the first scallop while allowing it to pass over the peaks and into the next scallop. Continue to make a full pass like this before flipping the knife over and stropping the back: flat or with a slight angle depending on how you deburred.

And that's how to sharpen a serrated knife. If you've raised and removed the burr as instructed, you should have a knife that glides through bread as if it were new!

Removing burr on a serrated knife

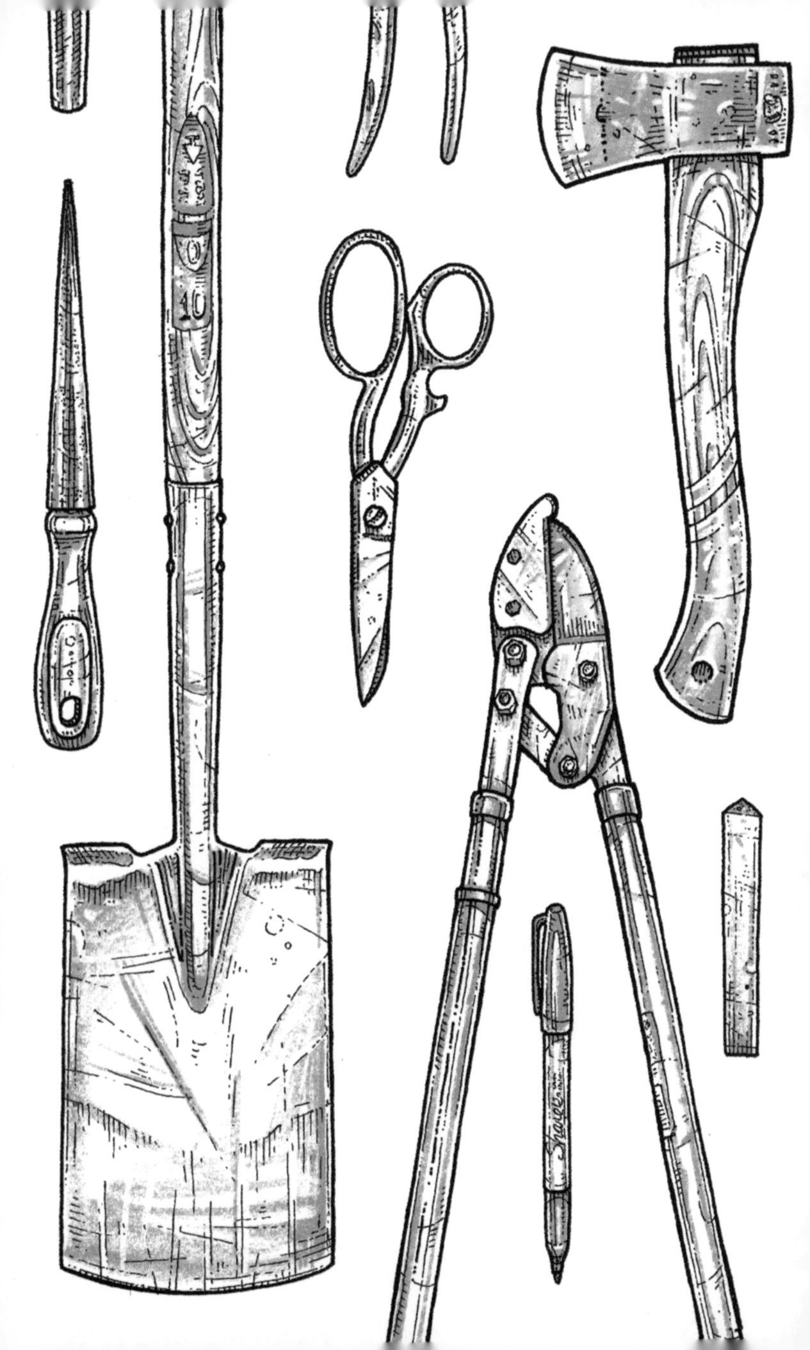

CHAPTER SIX

# Sharpening scissors, secateurs and other garden tools

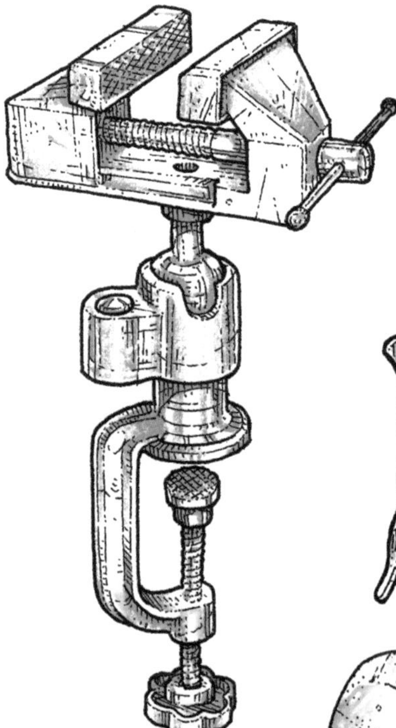

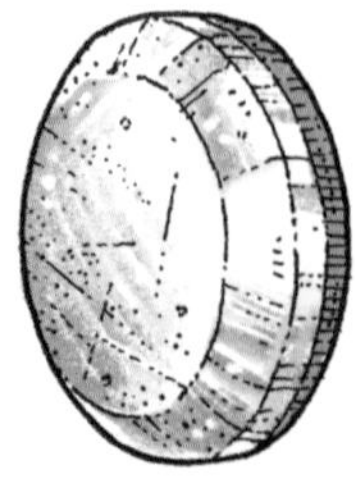

**Well done on conquering serrated knives. Now the bread knives can't hear us, I'm happy to tell you that serrated knives are my least favourite things to sharpen. Thankfully we tend to only have one or two!**

In this, our last chapter on sharpening, we're moving on to scissors and a few other items you'll use at home or in the garden. But don't fret, while the items themselves might be different, the methods aren't: scissors and shears are the same; loppers and secateurs are the same; and spades and edging irons are just like kitchen knives, the only major difference here is that we won't need the refining or stropping stages, so less work!

### What you will need

— **Diamond files**
— **A round or half-round engineer's file**
— **Triangular whetstone,** 10 × 1.3 cm (4 × ½ in), medium-grit
— **Puck whetstone**
— **Vice,** a small articulated one is best
— **Marker pen**
— **A couple of cloths**
— **A stable space to sharpen on,** e.g. kitchen worktop
— **Spray oil,** WD40 or equivalent

## Scissors and garden shears

Let's start by looking at the items with a shearing action: scissors and garden shears.

Unlike the items we've sharpened so far, shearing tools perform their cutting function at the point when two sharpened blades pass over each other.

For this cutting action to work, the edges of these blades need to be sharp—without flat spots along the apex—and they need to pass each other closely. If the pivot point—that's the screw or bolt which holds them together—is loose, then it will need addressing, as even when sharp it might prevent them from operating effectively.

With use, the apexes of the edges responsible for performing the cutting function become rounded out and dull, at which point the tool's functionality will begin to diminish. Ultimately, in the case of scissors, they will simply fold material or paper rather than cutting it.

**STEP 1**

### Preparing to sharpen

You'll be working on one blade at a time so clamp a single blade in your vice, with the outside facing towards you. Experiment with clamping the handle or the blade—my preference is the handle but you can't always get a solid grip because of the shape. If this is the case, then clamp the blade from the spine side with the bevel sticking up. At this point, for safety, I like to lay a cloth or pop a cork over the point of the blade which isn't being sharpened, to prevent any accidents. Next, take your marker pen and run it along the bevel—just the part that forms the cutting edge that you'll be removing material from. As with the serrated knives, this is going to help you find the angle.

Sharpening scissors

## STEP 2

### Find the sharpening angle

Next, with one of the blades clamped securely in the vice, take a file. If you're sharpening scissors use a diamond file; if sharpening garden shears, I prefer something more robust, like a round or half-round engineer's file.

Placing it on the bevel, as closely as you can to the existing angle, make a single stroke of the file, so it's moving away from your body, and lift off.

Now take a look at the bevel. If you've removed the pen marks across its whole width, then your angle is correct. If there is still some pen left across the inside of the bevel then you need to raise your file handle to correct the angle. If there is still some marker pen across the outside of the bevel, you need to lower the handle a little. Does that make sense? I hope so!

After making an adjustment, move along the bevel to repeat the process until you're happy that you're consistently removing pen marks from the entire width of the bevel. Now we've found our angle we can get sharpening.

## STEP 3

### Raising the burr

Maintaining the same angle, proceed and make passes across the whole bevel, making only single strokes away from you. Pulling the file back towards you can result in damage to the cutting edge, and increases the chances of you catching your hand on the blade. Repeat these strokes until you've raised a burr along its entire length.

Next, release the tool from the vice and, without closing the blades, flip them over, clamp in the other blade and repeat the entire process. Now you should have a pair of scissors or shears which are almost ready to return to active service... almost! The last thing we need to do is remove the burr.

### STEP 4

## Removing the burr

Unclamp your scissors or shears and, without closing them, place them on the work surface ready for deburring.

Taking your triangular whetstone, spray it with a few drops of oil and lie it flat on the inside of one of the blades; then lightly begin to move it along and down. What we're trying to do here is wear down the burr while minimising the amount we push over to the bevel side. So keep the strokes light and make several passes. Once it feels like the burr has all gone, have a quick feel of the bevel side to see if you've pushed any over. If you have, then make a light pass again on this side and then go back to the inside. Repeat this until it's all gone.

Finally, pop a tiny dot of oil around the pivot point of the scissors. If sharpening shears, give it a good spray. After that you're good to go!

Note: it's really important to ensure the triangular whetstone is completely flat. If you don't, there is a chance you could end up creating bevels on the inside of blades, and you really don't want that! It can be catastrophic for shearing tools, so make sure you keep the file flat.

I also alluded to the fact that you shouldn't close them once you've begun to create a burr. Shearing tools are finely engineered pieces of equipment, with the insides of the blades passing one another very closely and no room for extra bits of metal. So by not closing them once a burr has been raised, you avoid any chance of damage being done to the insides of the blades.

A final word: sometimes shears are only sharpened on one side, the bevel on the other side being flat and at a right angle to the inside of the blade. If this is the case, I recommend that you still work across this face and make sure this right angle is nice and crisp, without any damaged areas.

In a similar vein, sometimes scissors have small serrations on one side, particularly kitchen scissors, but often fabric scissors too. If you find that yours are like this, I would always err on the side of caution and recommend that you try to keep them as they were designed. So just sharpen the one side and see how they perform. If they still don't cut as you'd like, then consider working on the serrated side until you've sharpened the serrations out. I do this regularly with great success, but make a considered decision before jumping in. Finally, don't sharpen your hairdressing scissors this way. Get them done professionally.

Using a triangular whetstone to remove the burr

Sharpening secateurs

## Loppers and secateurs

In my opinion, the easiest things to sharpen are loppers and secateurs — not least they only have one blade! So, getting yours back into shape should take no time at all.

It's quite common for loppers and secateurs to have a secondary bevel, although sometimes they won't, in which case the primary bevel of the blade just runs right to the cutting edge. If it has a secondary bevel, then your sharpening angle wants to be the same as the angle of the bevel that's already there. If there isn't a secondary bevel, I recommend sharpening one in. They'll still be nice and sharp and will hopefully be a little more robust than if we tried to sharpen them at the angle of the original primary bevel.

**STEP 1**

### Preparing to sharpen

You've two options here, either clamp the handle in the vice so you've got good access to the bevel, or as I prefer, brace them in your hand as shown in the image. Go with whatever feels most natural to you.

**STEP 2**

### Finding the angle

There's a high chance your garden tools will be covered in patina. When this is worn away with the file, it will act like the marker pen did and highlight how close you are to the required sharpening angle. If they're stainless steel and have no patina, then mark up the bevel with the pen again first.

If the item you're sharpening has a secondary bevel, start by making a single stroke with the diamond file, as we did with the scissors. This is going to tell us how close our sharpening angle is to the angle of the bevel on the secateurs. If you've removed the patina across its whole width, then your angle is correct. If there is still some left across the inside of the bevel, then you need to raise the handle of the file to correct the angle. If there is still some marker pen across the outside of the bevel, you need to lower the handle a little. Adjust and experiment with the angle as necessary until the width of the material removed by your strokes matches the width of the existing bevel.

Secateurs that don't have secondary bevels are often Japanese-made and have a slightly convex primary bevel. We don't want to mess with this too much, but it can be difficult to do a good job of re-sharpening at this angle. So the addition of a secondary, almost micro-bevel can be a good solution. Around 23–25 degrees would be ideal, but again, it doesn't need to be perfect.

### STEP 3

## Raising and removing the burr

Having settled on the sharpening angle, place the top of your file on the bevel, just above the pivot point (the bolt which holds them together). Apply pressure and make one continuous stroke, simultaneously moving the file down and across the blade. Aim to get to the tip of the blade at the same time as the bottom of the file, or make sure you restart where you finished if you don't manage to make a complete stroke.

Repeat this action as many times as necessary until you've raised a burr across the inside of the blade.

Once a burr has been raised you then need to carefully remove it from the inside of the blade in the same way as with scissors. Taking your triangular whetstone, lie it

Removing the burr with a triangular whetstone

flat on the inside of the blade and lightly begin to move it along. What we're trying to do here is to wear down the burr while minimising the amount we push over to the bevel side. So, keep the strokes light and make several passes. Once it feels like the burr has all gone, have a quick feel of the bevel side to see if you've pushed any over. If you have, then make a light pass again on this side and then go back to the inside, repeating this until it's all gone.

And, like with the scissors, keep the whetstone flat against the bevel while deburring, so as not to create a bevel on the inside of the blade.

Finally, give them a nice squirt of oil, tighten the bolt at the pivot point if needed, and you're all done!

## Spades and edging irons

Okay, so maybe you're wondering why on earth anyone would bother to sharpen a garden spade—I do agree, they definitely shouldn't be top of your sharpening list. But nonetheless, a sharp spade is going to be much easier to use than a blunt one, especially when working in rooty ground, so it's worth the effort.

### STEP 1

### Preparing to sharpen

I recommend the use of a coarse engineer's file again, preferably a half-round file. For this job you're going to be removing a fair bit more material than when sharpening any of the other items.

Start by clamping the tool in your vice so the blade is facing up. If the tool is too big for your vice, you'll likely be better to lie it over a chair and sit with the handle between your legs and the blade sticking out, so you're working right in front of you (pictured overleaf).

STEP 2

## Finding the angle

We're going to sharpen at an approximate 45-degree angle but, this time, the angle really isn't important. You're just trying to reunify both sides of the edge by removing some material and thus create a new apex. Rough is absolutely fine here, just err on the side of a high rather than low angle. The work it's going to be doing is heavy and a very sharp edge will roll over in no time at all.

To find your approximate 45 degrees, place your file across the edge of the spade at a 90-degree angle and then lower the handle by roughly half.

STEP 3

## Raising and removing the burr

Applying pressure to the top side of your file, begin to make careful strokes away from your body, simultaneously travelling along the edge of the spade while making strokes down the file. Don't try to travel the whole length of the bevel with each stroke this time though, it's far too long and you likely won't manage it. Just break it down into a few sections and work on a bit at a time.

Once you reach the end of the file, rather than pulling it back to you and attempting to remove material on the return stroke, lift it off and repeat the process, making the full pass with push strokes. In my experience the coarse file can easily get jammed on the bevel, increasing the chance of slipping while pulling the file towards you and causing an injury, so be careful.

Sharpening a spade

Repeat these strokes along the whole edge of the spade or edging iron, turning it over and alternating back and forth between sides until a burr has been raised.

Once raised, make a few light passes with your file and remove as much of the burr as you can. But, just like with the angle, perfection is far from important here, just tidy it up a bit!

## Axes

The edge of an axe is something that takes a real beating, especially if it's being used to chop wood on an inappropriate surface, like directly onto a concrete floor.

**STEP 1**

### Preparing to sharpen

First off, you're going to need your vice again. One option might be to clamp the axe between your legs (useful if you're out in the field), but if you've got the vice, why not get your money's worth — it makes the job easier too.

Next, take a look at the bevel of your axe. You might find that it has a bevel with a straight side, or you might find that it has it has a convex edge. Now you've identified this you can colour in the bevel with your marker.

**STEP 2**

### Finding the angle

Clamp the axe firmly in your vice, either by the butt (flat end of the blade, opposite the cutting edge) or the handle if it's a small-bladed axe like a hatchet. Take your file or puck whetstone. Go for a large half-round file if you're going to need to remove a decent amount of material; a finer file is okay if it's just a touch-up. Next, with your file, make a push stroke along the bevel (lift the file off when you bring it back towards you to avoid pulling your hand into the cutting edge), take a look and ensure you've removed the pen right up to the cutting edge. If you haven't, lower or raise your sharpening angle accordingly and repeat the test stroke until you've found the correct sharpening angle.

If your axe has a convex edge, the file strokes you make will need to follow this shape, so you'll be moving the file towards the edge in an arc. If the bevel is straight-sided, you'll need to keep the file as close to the angle of the bevel as possible. Keep an eye on the marker throughout to make sure that you're sticking with the correct angle.

### STEP 3

## Raising and removing the burr

Repeat this action on alternating sides, removing the axe from the vice and repositioning each time until you've raised a burr. At which point, I recommend making several more alternating strokes but with a much lighter pressure, until the burr has been worn away.

You should be left with a sharp axe — sharp enough to tackle splitting and kindling without any issue — but it won't be a very refined finish. Of course, axes can be refined much more than this, and I'm into it! I'd recommend swapping out the files for a puck whetstone. This is a combination whetstone like we used for knives, but round and small enough to be able to be picked up and used in the hand. Start with the coarse side and use it in a circular motion across the edge of the axe until you raise a burr, then flip to your medium-grit side for a much finer finish.

Sharpening an axe

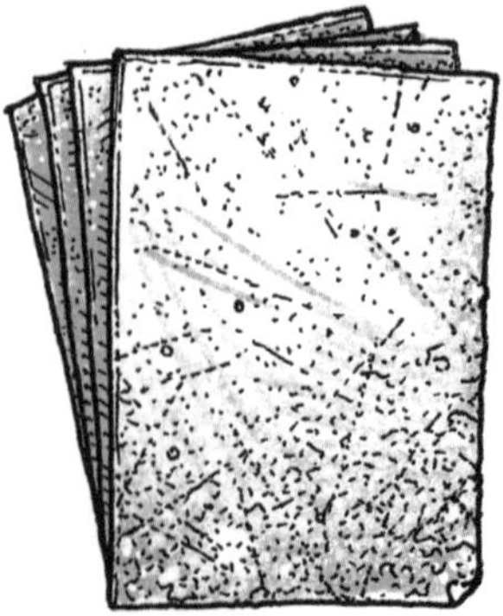

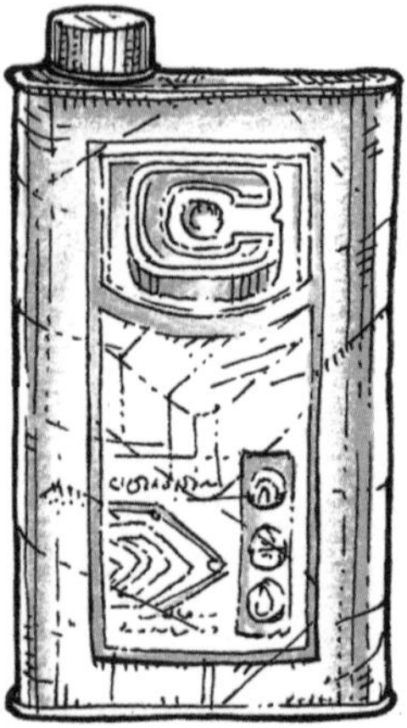

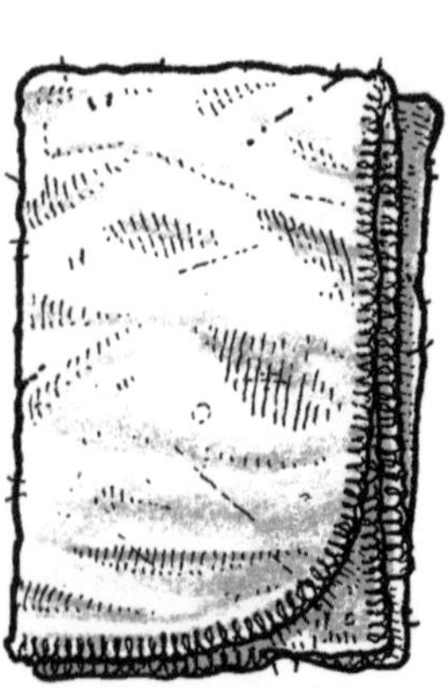

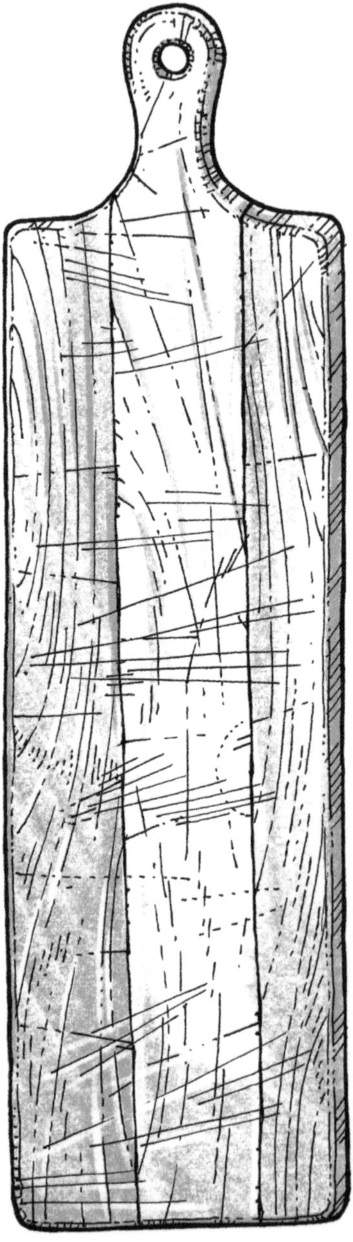

CHAPTER SEVEN

# Treating wooden boards and seasoning pans

**In this chapter, we're going to look at a few other kitchen maintenance tasks, not related to sharpening but important nonetheless!**

What you will need

— **Wood oil or wood wax** for boards and handles
— **Rapeseed oil** for pans
— **A cloth**
— **Medium-grit sandpaper**

## Wooden handles and chopping boards

Dry wooden handles and dry boards are easily neglected, as they don't cause quite as many frustrations as a blunt knife. However, they have a much higher chance of splitting and breaking, and are prone to staining and soaking up liquids they come into contact with. Neglected wood can look ugly and feel rough to the touch, and have a higher chance of shedding small bits of wood into your food. Thankfully, it's an easy fix. You're just going to need some food-safe oil or wax and a cloth to apply it.

My preferred oil for chopping boards is called tung oil.

It's a viscous oil that takes a little time to dry but it leaves a lovely finish. Walnut oil is also highly recommended and there are other options out there too. Although best to avoid both if you have a nut allergy!

For handles, wooden spoons and chopsticks, I tend to favour a beeswax-based blend, designed specifically for this purpose.

Whichever oil or wax you choose, it's essential that you check that it's marked as food-safe. There might be several preparations under the same name, some of which might be food-safe and some not, so don't get caught out. It's also worth noting that you can't just pour your cooking oil onto your chopping board. Most common cooking oils are likely to go rancid on your board over time and would start to smell.

So, once you've got your oil or wax of choice, it's as simple as pouring or wiping a little onto a cloth and rubbing it onto your board or handle. I recommend applying a liberal amount, letting it sit for a good few hours (or overnight) and then wiping off the excess with a clean, dry cloth. Once oiled you should find that water and other liquids run off rather than soaking in — and it feels much smoother to the touch.

Before you start, if you find that your chopping board is very rough, it might be a good idea to start by giving it a light sand. This will get rid of most of the texture, helping you to achieve a smoother finish in the end. Just make sure you thoroughly remove any dust created in the process before you start oiling.

A final note on washing wooden items. Putting them in the dishwasher will dry them out something daft. It will quickly cause knife handles to crack and chopping boards to warp, so don't be tempted! Also, for the same reason, it's best to avoid drying them on radiators.

Oiling a wooden chopping board

## Cast-iron and carbon steel cookware

We love carbon steel and cast-iron pans, especially when it comes to frying. The evenness of heat, the weight in your hand, the aesthetic, all make them a dream to use in the kitchen.

In a similar way to the frustrations caused by blunt knives, have you had the experience of frying something on the hob and it sticks? You get frustrated when you can't make a decent pancake, so you buy a new pan. You're careful but somehow it picks up a scratch and you end up replacing it again in 18 months. It's a story we hear all the time, and something we used to experience ourselves until we switched to a carbon steel frying pan.

A common misconception is that they are not non-stick, but there is a non-stick coating on carbon steel and cast-iron pans. They can perform just as well as a brand new, top-of-the-range non-stick pan. But this coating is made from vegetable oil, not Teflon (which has had some heavy criticism in recent years over various health concerns related to its use) and it's put there by you, so can be refreshed again and again and again, pretty much indefinitely. So, if you get hold of a good-quality pan made from carbon steel or cast iron and look after it properly, it will be the last one you ever need to buy. Just think of that!

This process of creating a non-stick coating is called 'polymerisation' and happens when a layer of oil on the surface of the pan is heated to a hot enough temperature, for a long enough time, at which point it changes from a liquid to a solid, bonded to and coating the surface of your pan. In turn, creating a brand new, beautifully non-stick surface for you to fry on. Who knew?!

And because it's replaceable, you don't need to be precious about it. Use whichever utensils you like, make the pan work for you without worrying about hurting its feelings like you have to with all the non-stick versions you've had in the past.

Getting this lovely fresh non-stick layer on your pan is called seasoning.

## How to season your pan

Give the pan a clean, scrub it well with some soap and warm water and make sure you've got rid of all the texture from tiny bits of food stuck to the surface.

Next, make sure it's properly dry before applying a *very* thin layer of oil to the surface both inside and outside. I recommend rapeseed oil and use a piece of kitchen roll or the corner of a tea towel to apply it. Too much oil and it will drip and pool—you want just enough so you can see it glistening in the light. Next, pop it into a cold oven, on the middle shelf, upside down.

Turn the oven on to a medium heat (approx. 180°C / 350°F) and leave for 15–20 minutes before turning up to approximately 250°C / 480°F).

Leave for around an hour before turning the oven off and, without removing the pan, allow it to cool. The process will continue while the pan is cooling. It also prevents anyone from grabbing the handle of a red-hot pan. I've done this and it's awful! As the pan is heavy, you naturally get a good grip—need I say more. If you do need to take it out of the oven before it's cooled, it's absolutely essential that you use an oven glove or a folded towel over the handle and proceed with caution.

Once it's cooled, you're good to go. Use your pan, enjoy it and season it again when needed.

And you'll know when it's needed because things start sticking again! We re-season ours about three times a year.

Seasoning a carbon steel pan

CHAPTER EIGHT

# Step-by-step guides

**So, by now you've been through all the instructional chapters in the book and you're familiar with how to sharpen your knives, scissors and tools. But how the hell are you actually going to sharpen them when life is busy and you don't have time to take on any more new jobs?**

Well, as much as we might struggle to find the time for new things like this, find it we must, because these babies aren't going to sharpen themselves.

Initially, particularly when it comes to the kitchen knives, there's going to be quite a steep learning curve. During this period, the task will take longer to complete than when you're at the top of the curve. So remember, just because a knife might take you half an hour to sharpen today, that doesn't mean it will always take that long. Don't be disheartened and give up because you think it's going to take hours and hours each time, because that really isn't the case.

In the first instance, my advice is to set aside an afternoon or evening and go through the steps in the relevant chapter without any expectations or pressure. Take your time and familiarise yourself with the entire process. Read and re-read the steps, look at the pictures, learn how to hold the knife or the file, experiment with how much pressure to use.

Spend as much time as you need to get your first knife sharpened. Don't expect it to be done in five minutes, and don't expect to get through a dozen knives in your first session. We want you to do a good job here, good enough so you want to tell people about what you did and show them how sharp you got your knives. This is going to be far more instrumental in helping you build a sustainable sharpening practice than it would by half-arsing your way through a dozen knives. Once you've got through your first knife and you're happy with it, if you've still some time and motivation left, have a crack at another. Then keep carving out an hour here and there until you've got through them all. And really nail finding the burr!

Once you're at this stage, I'd recommend just listening to your knives—yes, listening to your knives!—and getting feedback from them. As soon as they stop responding well to the strop and cease to cut like you want, it's time to soak the stone again. Only this time it will be a much quicker job because you'll be more practised, more efficient and will have knives in a way better state of repair than last time around. Win-win!

As for the other items we've covered in the book, they all require less effort to maintain than kitchen knives. But you will still need to allocate a bit more time in the early stages to familiarise yourself with the techniques and the sequence involved.

So, the rest of this chapter is going to be dedicated to quick reference guides. These bullet points aim to chaperone you through each job, giving you an easy reference once you're familiar with the process. I strongly recommend you go through the detailed steps outlined in each relevant chapter until you're comfortable with them.

## Knives

1. Assess knife's requirements and choose foundation whetstone
2. Soak whetstone
3. Assume correct sharpening position
4. Find angle
5. Carry out 2 alternating passes on each side at full pressure
6. Assess for burr and consistency of bevel
7. Continue to make alternating passes until burr has been raised along entire length of knife; adjust angle if bevel is inconsistent or smaller / bigger than expected
8. Make 2 alternating light-pressure passes on each side and assess burr, if still present then repeat, if not, move on
9. Make 2 alternating passes on each side of edge-trailing strokes
10. Move on to next stone in progression (i.e. medium-grit stone if you've just finished on low-grit stone) and repeat steps 3–9
11. Strop knife with edge-trailing strokes, 6 alternating passes on each side

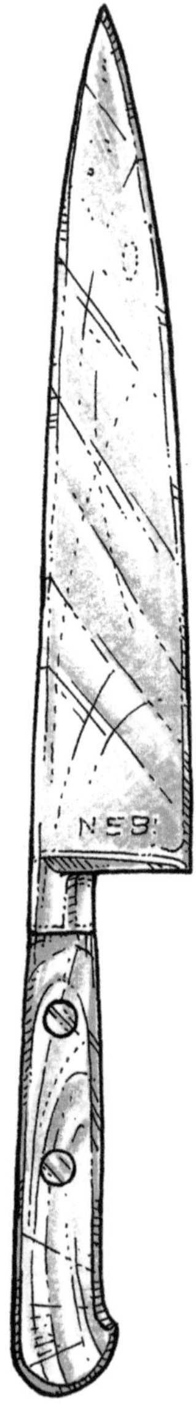

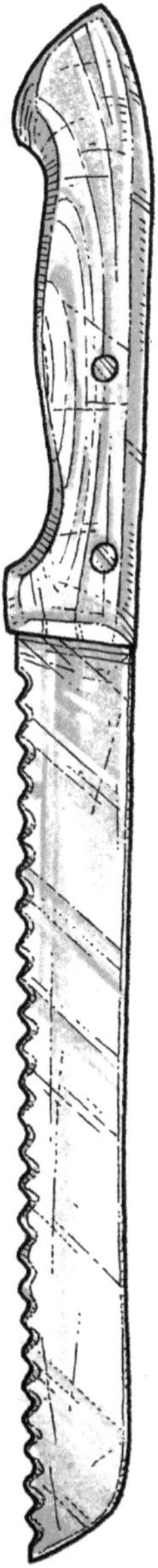

## Serrated knives

1. Clamp knife in vice and soak whetstone
2. Assess knife and decide whether to sharpen at original angle or add micro-bevel
3. Mark the bevel with marker pen
4. With a file, make several test strokes to assess angle by observing amount of pen removed
5. Correct angle as needed
6. Work between each scallop at desired angle until burr has been raised across the back side of knife
7. Decide whether to deburr with knife flat or whether to add a slight bevel to back of knife
8. Remove burr
9. Strop

## Scissors and garden shears

1. Clamp item in vice
2. Colour in bevels with marker pen
3. Make several test strokes with file and assess angle by observing pen marks removed by this action
4. Correct angle as needed
5. Continue to make push strokes across surface of bevel at correct angle, until burr has been raised across entire length
6. Unclamp, remove from vice and re-clamp second blade
7. Repeat steps 3–5
8. Remove from vice and carefully deburr by running file flat across the inside of blade; continue until burr has been completely removed
9. Carefully run triangular whetstone flat across the bevel again, then across the inside to remove any last sections of burr
10. Repeat on the second blade

## Loppers and secateurs

1. Brace item well in your hand or clamp in vice
2. Make test stroke to assess sharpening angle, adjust if necessary
3. Sharpen across entire length of blade using push strokes
4. Continue until burr has been raised
5. With file flat across the back, make strokes along the entire length of blade until burr is completely removed
6. Carefully run triangular whetstone flat across the bevel again, then across the burr side to remove any last sections of burr which might have been pushed over during first deburring

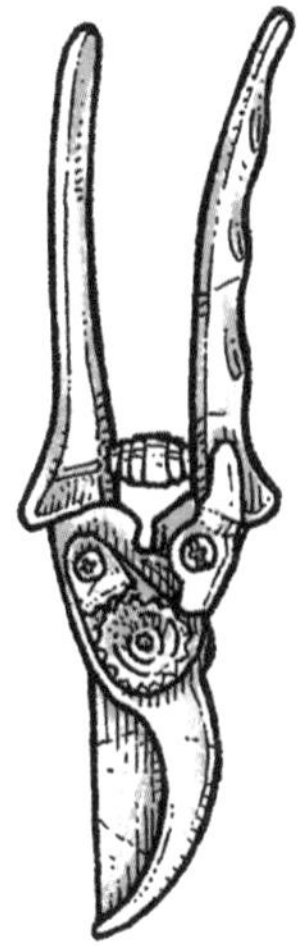

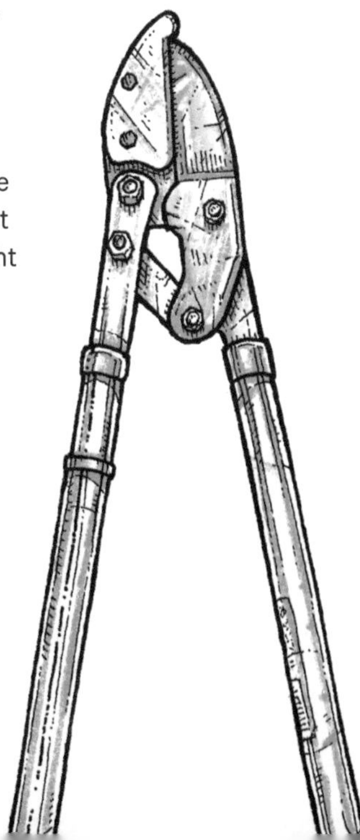

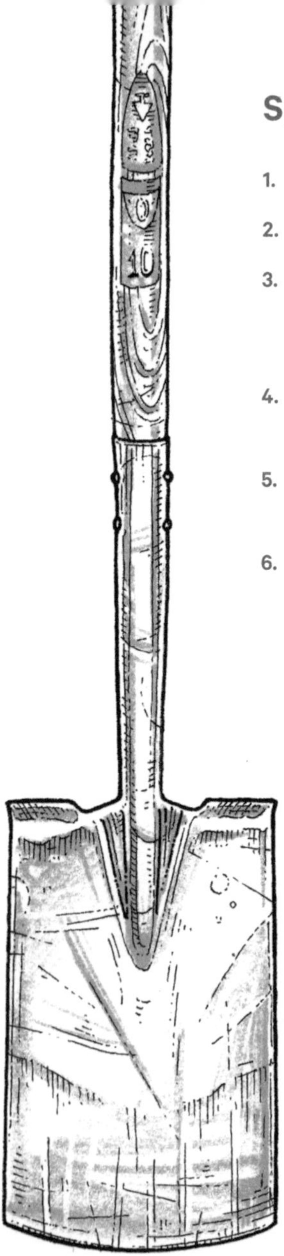


## Spades and edging irons

1. Clamp or secure item
2. Find sharpening angle
3. Make 2 alternating passes with push strokes across each side of the edge
4. Take a look at the bevel and see if you've raised a burr
5. Continue repeating steps 2 and 3 until you've raised a burr
6. Make a few light passes to reduce the burr (although there's no need to worry too much about making sure it's all gone on a tool such as this)

## Axes

1. Clamp in vice
2. Check whether your axe has a straight or a convex bevel
3. Following the bevel, use file to make push strokes over cutting edge, lift file and reset to original position, rather than making a pull stroke
4. Repeat along length of edge, alternating each side until burr is raised
5. Remove burr with light-pressure strokes

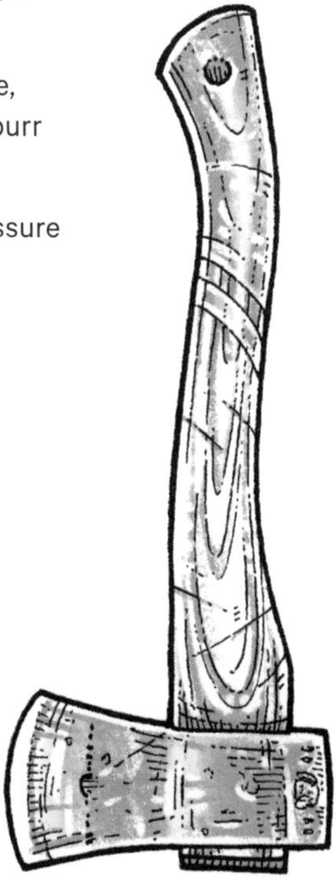

刃物椿
TARIST

CHAPTER NINE

# The philosophy of maintenance

**By this point you've probably, at the very least, had a go at sharpening. Some of you may have gone all out and sharpened every knife and tool you own.**

As you're learning a new skill, the demands on your concentration are high—you need to follow instructions closely, count strokes and passes, and carefully inspect your work. But as time goes by and you become more comfortable with the process, you'll find that a lot of this starts to become second nature. You can call upon yourself to intervene and make decisions, but the majority of the work is done from muscle memory.

It's when you get to this stage that you can start to discover sharpening's hidden benefits! At the beginning of the book we talked about how having a sharp knife can be beneficial when you're cooking, for example, but how can the actual act of sharpening benefit you while you're doing it?

At its most basic level, sharpening is an activity. It's not climbing a mountain or running a marathon, but it is getting you out of the chair and (albeit mildly) active. And if you're someone who likes the chair, then this is an improvement, so good work!

In my opinion, one of the big benefits of sharpening is that it entertains your hands and focuses your mind.

Of course, you do have the option of popping on the telly, some music or a podcast while you're working, but in the beginning at least I wholeheartedly encourage you to immerse yourself fully in the process and take the opportunity to have a break from external distractions. We're so used to feeding our brain with a constant supply of tasty morsels that, if treated right, your sharpening sessions can become a bit of a haven of solitude.

So when it comes time for you to sharpen, I encourage you to engage in the ceremonial nature of the process. Take time to set out your work area, place your stones and strop out in a row, arrange your knives or tools to be sharpened on a cloth to your left, and, once sharpened, place them on a cloth on your right. Designate a particular apron to the task in hand (I like to wear a chore jacket I've named my sharpening jacket). But really, just think about what you're doing and be intentional. A practical activity like this will never be a substitute for something as powerful as, say, meditation, but if you engage with the process and minimise external distractions you can quickly discover the mindful nature of sharpening.

If you do manage to cultivate this type of attitude towards sharpening, it becomes possible to double the return on your investment of time. You've got the outcome —the sharp knives you originally came for—but you've also got the practice itself. And who's to say this isn't the real benefit of sharpening?

Back in Chapter 1, we covered why we should be maintaining our knives and tools. Hopefully I presented a compelling argument in favour of doing so. Now we're a little way down the line and maybe you've had the pleasure of using your newly sharpened items, experienced the benefits first-hand, and have realised how much better your knife performs!

So while you're here, with your fresh outlook on life, I wonder if it's worth seeing if we can apply these newfound principles to any other aspects of it? Do we own any other things which would benefit from or perform better after some TLC?

An obvious place to start is with our clothes, do we own any items that could have their useful lives extended after just a little work? Could sewing on a few buttons decrease our frustrations and spare the blushes of our colleagues?

What about cleaning out the filters on the washing machine, the hoover, the dehumidifier? I'm sure they would all work better if they were taken care of. Pumping up the tyres on your car might improve your fuel consumption by a few per cent, while deleting the unused apps or nonsense photos off your phone might prevent you having to buy more storage space.

And these are just some of the physical things. What about maintaining relationships? The older we get, the less time we make to see our friends, even our partners. Making the effort every now and then might work wonders for you both.

And as Chance writes so eloquently in this book's foreword, let's not forget the relationship with ourselves and our own mental maintenance: 'It's about doing something small that points to something big.' And doing it with some regularity, rather than waiting until it's broken.

# Conclusion

**We've reached the end, well done, us! I don't imagine that this is the first book you've ever read, but it's the first one I've written, and I really appreciate you reading it!**

Sharpening, as I'm sure you can tell, is something I'm extremely passionate about and I'm confident that, given half a chance, you will be too.

Well done for learning new skills and forming new habits. In a world with so many distractions it isn't easy, but following through with this really is worth it. There is great potential for positive change when you become a sharpener and all-round maintainer!

By carrying out the simple tasks outlined in this book, you'll lighten the financial load associated with paying for someone else to sharpen for you, or from constantly replacing worn-out items, which will also reduce your environmental footprint.

I'd also like to encourage you to acknowledge the sense of pride that work like this brings. That knife was rubbish and now it's not, and you did it! You've engaged in a practice that has been carried out this way for thousands of years, and you used it to sharpen your knives, good job!

I sincerely wish you the best of luck on your sharpening and maintaining journey. Thanks again for reading, strop every time you use your knife, sharpen when needed and —let's all say it together—make sure you find the burr!

Sharpening a kitchen knife on a medium-grit whetstone

# Glossary of terms

**Abrasives:** Items or materials used to wear material off, or shape another item.

**Angle:** The space between two intersecting lines, measured in degrees.

**Apex:** The very top of the cutting edge, the point where both sides of a bevel meet.

**Belly:** Curved section of cutting edge.

**Bevel:** Angled surface of knife or cutting tool.

**Blade:** The knife as a whole; when you hold the handle, the rest is the blade.

**Blunt:** An edge in a bad state of repair, that has lost sharpness.

**Bolster:** Chunky, reinforced section between blade and handle of a traditional Western kitchen knife.

**Burr:** Lip of metal pushed over the apex when both sides of cutting edge have been reunified during sharpening.

**Choil:** Section of knife blade between heel and handle, where fingers rest during use.

**Combination whetstone:** A whetstone comprised of two whetstones with different grits, bonded back-to-back.

**Convex bevel:** Bevel which is slightly curved outwards.

**Cutting edge:** Business end of the knife, the part which cuts.

**Diamond file:** Abrasive tool covered with industrial-grade diamonds, for removal of metal.

**Edge-leading:** A sharpening stroke across the whetstone with cutting edge in front of the movement.

**Edge-trailing:** A sharpening stroke across the whetstone, with cutting edge behind the movement.

**Engineer's file:** Abrasive steel tool for removal of metal.

**Geometrical sharpness:** How thick or thin a knife is behind the cutting edge.

**Grit (coarse, medium, fine):** Size of the abrasive particles which make up a particular whetstone.

**Heel:** Section of knife where the cutting edge ends; the intersection with choil or bolster.

**Lapping stone:** Used to flatten a whetstone.

**Primary bevel:** The angled sides of a knife, tapered from spine to secondary bevel.

**Puck whetstone:** Palm-sized whetstone for sharpening axes.

**Retractable diamond pen file:** Small abrasive tool covered with industrial-grade diamonds, shaped similar to a pen; retracts into its own casing. For removal of metal.

**Rivets:** Metal pins to hold knife handle together.

**Rolled edge:** Early stages of bluntness, where the apex of the cutting edge has been pushed over to one side.

**Scales:** Wood, resin or plastic sheet material used to flank the tang to form a handle on a Western kitchen knife.

**Seasoning:** Layer applied to carbon steel or cast-iron pan to form non-stick coating.

**Secondary bevel:** Angled section of knife which makes up the cutting edge; the area you'll be working on when sharpening a knife.

**Serrations:** Sharp pointed teeth, separated by bevelled crescents on a serrated knife.

**Scallops:** Gentler, more rounded teeth, separated by bevelled crescents on a serrated knife.

**Spine:** Part of knife which faces up during use, opposite the cutting edge.

**Strop:** Smooth surface used to keep a knife sharp.

**Tang:** The part of the knife blade which is inside the handle.

**Tip:** The very end of the knife, where cutting edge and spine meet.

**Vice:** Tool for gripping and holding steady items to be worked on.

**Whetstone:** Abrasive block used for sharpening.

# About the author

Gareth Heaton lives and works in Ilkley, West Yorkshire, with his long-term partner Georgina and their whippet, Mookie. Between them they own and run Community Cutlery, a kitchenware business specialising in the retail and sharpening of kitchen knives.

Sharpening professionally since 2019, Gareth has sharpened tens of thousands of knives, for domestic and professional users, both in his workshop and at various locations around the UK. After discovering there was a huge appetite for learning, Gareth has gone on to teach many people how to sharpen their own knives and tools, in person and online.

You can find Gareth at *communitycutlery.co.uk* and on social media *@communitycutlery*

# Thanks

To everyone who bought or read this book: the world needs more maintainers.

All the sharpeners and craftspeople who have taught me along the way: Matt from American Edge for providing the spark that started this whole thing. Scott from *@sheffield_knife_sharpening*, Tom *@burnt_orchid*, Pete *@the_sharpen_shack*, Simon *@simonchefknife*, Steve *@Rockchopknifeco*, Michael *@waterhouse.england*, Josh *@Bernalcutlery*, Vincent *@vincentsavesknives*, Murray *@cartercutlery*, Ricky *@rykytran*, Peter *@soulwood_creations*, to name but a few.

Dad, Uncle Paul, Grandad and everyone else who has taught me anything practical over the years.

The DO Lectures family, especially Ilya Romain for getting me in the door.

Miranda, Jess and Anya at Do Books; how I was ever allowed to write a book will be beyond confusing for the English teachers from my past. Thanks for believing in me and this project. Also to Lee, Chez, Joan, Wilf and James for your great work on this book.

Chance Marshall for your excellent intro to this book and championing us every step of the way.

Neil and Melanie Kirkbride at The Soft Road for your support and direction.

Dave and Joy for all your support and encouragement.

Mum, Vict, Paddy, Geoff, Ella and Patchy for everything, especially for being a right laugh, I love you all.

And of course, to George, to Gina, to Gene, to Bean, to Baff, for your support throughout this project, for believing in me, for holding the fort while I've been writing, for providing the hand-written labels and arrows, and for absolutely everything else, I love you.

## Books in the series

**Do Agile** Tim Drake
**Do Beekeeping** Orren Fox
**Do Birth** Caroline Flint
**Do Bitcoin** Angelo Morgan-Somers
**Do Blue** Nick Hounsfield & Abby Richardson
**Do Breathe** Michael Townsend Williams
**Do Build** Alan Moore
**Do Conversation** Robert Poynton
**Do Deal** Richard Hoare & Andrew Gummer
**Do Death** Amanda Blainey
**Do Design** Alan Moore
**Do Disrupt** Mark Shayler
**Do Drama** Lucy Gannon
**Do Earth** Tam Omond
**Do Ferment** Matthew Pennington & Nicola Cradock
**Do Fly** Gavin Strange
**Do Grow** Alice Holden
**Do Hope** Gail Muller
**Do Improvise** Robert Poynton
**Do Inhabit** Sue Fan & Danielle Quigley
**Do Interesting** Russell Davies
**Do Lead** Les McKeown
**Do Listen** Bobette Buster
**Do Loss** Sue Deagle
**Do Maintain** Gareth Heaton
**Do Make** James Otter
**Do Nourish** Sarah Bayliss
**Do Open** David Hieatt
**Do Pause** Robert Poynton
**Do Photo** Andrew Paynter
**Do Present** Mark Shayler
**Do Preserve** Anja Dunk, Jen Goss & Mimi Beaven
**Do Protect** Johnathan Rees
**Do Purpose** David Hieatt
**Do Recruit** Khalilah Olokunola
**Do Reset** Jillian Lavender
**Do Scale** Les McKeown
**Do Sea Salt** Alison, David & Jess Lea-Wilson
**Do Sing** James Sills
**Do Smoke** Jen Goss & Scott Davis
**Do Sourdough** Andrew Whitley
**Do Start** Dan Kieran
**Do Story** Bobette Buster
**Do Team** Charlie Gladstone
**Do Walk** Libby DeLana
**Do Wild Baking** Tom Herbert

## Also available

**The Book of Do** ed. Miranda West
**Path** Louisa Thomsen Brits
**The Skimming Stone** Dominic Wilcox
**Stay Curious** Clare Hieatt
**The Path of a Doer** David Hieatt

Available in print, digital and audio formats from booksellers or via our website: **thedobook.co**. To hear about events and forthcoming titles, find us on social media **@dobookco**, or subscribe to our newsletter.